ROUTLEDGE LIBRARY EDITIONS: DEMOGRAPHY

Volume 2

FULL HOUSE

FULL HOUSE

Reassessing the Earth's Population Carrying Capacity

LESTER R. BROWN
AND
HAL KANE

Routledge
Taylor & Francis Group

LONDON AND NEW YORK

First published in 1995 by Earthscan Publications Ltd.

This edition first published in 2024
by Routledge
4 Park Square, Milton Park, Abingdon, Oxon OX14 4RN

and by Routledge
605 Third Avenue, New York, NY 10158

Routledge is an imprint of the Taylor & Francis Group, an informa business

British Library Cataloguing in Publication Data
A catalogue record for this book is available from the British Library

ISBN: 978-1-032-53819-8 (Set)
ISBN: 978-1-032-54840-1 (Volume 2) (hbk)
ISBN: 978-1-032-54841-8 (Volume 2) (pbk)
ISBN: 978-1-003-42772-8 (Volume 2) (ebk)

DOI: 10.4324/9781003427728

Publisher's Note
The publisher has gone to great lengths to ensure the quality of this reprint but points out that some imperfections in the original copies may be apparent.

Disclaimer
The publisher has made every effort to trace copyright holders and would welcome correspondence from those they have been unable to trace.

Full House

Reassessing the Earth's Population Carrying Capacity

EARTHSCAN

Earthscan Publications Ltd, London

First published 1995 by
Earthscan Publications Limited
120 Pentonville Road, London N1 9JN

British Library Cataloguing-in-Publication Data

A catalogue record for this book is available from the British Library

ISBN 1 85383 251 0

Printed by Biddles Ltd, Guildford and Kings Lynn.

Earthscan Publications Limited is an editorially independent
subsidiary of Kogan Page Limited and publishes in association
with the International Institute for Environment and
Development and the World Wide Fund for Nature.

Contents

Acknowledgments

This book should be seen as a continuation of work on food and carrying capacity done over the years at the Institute. It draws on earlier editions of our *State of the World* and *Vital Signs* annual reports as well as selected Worldwatch Papers. In addition to being grateful to those who worked on these publications, we are particularly indebted to Reah Janise Kauffman, who worked tirelessly to produce fresh drafts in rapid succession. Her commitment to the project helped complete it in record time. Elena Wilken helped in the review stages, critiquing ideas and checking details.

Linda Starke brought her unparalleled talents to bear on the manuscript as editor and production coordinator. We appreciate her efficiency, which permitted a quick turnaround, and her familiarity with the issues, which improved the quality of the manuscript.

Several people inside and outside the Institute took time out of busy schedules to review all or part of the manuscript. In addition to our colleagues at Worldwatch, we want to thank Tim Atkeson, Laurie Burnham, Dana Dalrymple, Herman Daly, Nurul Islam, William Mansfield, Michel Petit, Joe Speidel, and Robert Wallace for their reviews.

In this work, we drew heavily on the world agricultural database of the U.S. Department of Agriculture. This resource was particularly useful because of its long-term historical perspective, providing data for all countries back to 1950. We are particularly grateful to individuals at the Economic Research Service who responded to our many requests for further information.

Francis Urban and Ray Nightingale's organization of world demographic data originally produced by the international division of the U.S. Bureau of the Census was especially helpful. The convenience of having a well-organized demographic database that provided historical data as well as long-term projections for all countries was invaluable.

We would like to thank the Turner Foundation, which supported the research on carrying capacity that is incorporated in this book. The deep personal committment of Ted Turner and Jane Fonda to population and environmental issues encouraged us to undertake this project. We are also indebted to the Wallace Genetic Foundation, which provided specific support for this project and where the three trustees—Robert B. Wallace, Jean Wallace Douglas, and Henry B. Wallace—all have a longstanding interest in food and population. Also supporting this project is the McBride Family Fund, where John McBride has a keen interest in population issues. Others that support the Institute's work include the Geraldine R. Dodge, Ford, W. Alton Jones, John and Catherine T. MacArthur, Andrew W. Mellon, Edward John Noble, Surdna, and Frank Weeden foundations; the Pew Memorial Trust; and the Prickett and Rockefeller Brothers funds. Peter Buckley has provided a personal grant for general support.

Our colleagues at W.W. Norton & Company, Andrew Marasia and Iva Ashner, helped make a tight timetable work. We are indebted to them for publishing all our books, and particularly for their support of this Environmental Alert Series.

We have drawn on the work of many researchers in many different fields in doing this book, and we are grateful to them. Our goal here is to raise the level of interest and understanding of a set of issues that we think is getting all too little attention. We hope that this volume will encourage many national governments to undertake their own carrying capacity assessments, incorporating the latest information available to them.

Lester R. Brown
Hal Kane

Worldwatch Institute
1776 Massachusetts Ave., N.W.
Washington, D.C. 20036

June 1994

Editor's Note

The first time I heard Lester Brown talk about population, he was addressing an audience of very enthused, very concerned participants at a nongovernmental forum held during the U.N. World Population Conference in Bucharest. The year was 1974. And the debate of the day was whether the emphasis should be on family planning or development.

Twenty years later, the United Nations is again holding a global conference on population, this time in Cairo. By now, it is clear that family planning and development—education, a chance to earn a living, equal opportunites for women, and so on—reinforce each other. And this is reflected in the 1994 meeting's title: the International Conference on Population and Development.

In between these two meetings, Lester Brown has continued to write about the connections between population growth and socioeconomic development. Hal Kane has studied and written about the imperative of sustainable development. They have both looked at the bigger picture of mounting pressures on our life-support systems. In *Full House*, Lester and Hal consider the most basic issue raised by the unrelenting growth of population: how many people can the earth support, and at what level of consumption? No more important question challenges scientists, policymakers, and every one of us than this.

Full House is the fourth book in the Worldwatch Environmental Alert Series, published in time for the U.N. Conference in Cairo. Earlier books in the series are *Saving the Planet*, on the strategies needed for an environmentally sustainable global economy; *How Much Is Enough?*, on taming consumerism and searching for sufficiency in our life-styles; and *Last Oasis*, on growing water scarcity and the need to invest in water efficiency. Hot on the heels of this book is *Power Surge*, a guide to the coming energy revolution by Christopher Flavin and Nicholas Lenssen.

We hope these short, lively volumes on specific issues, in combination with Worldwatch's annual books *State of the World* and *Vital Signs*, can make a small contribution to building a sustainable world. Your comments and ideas for future topics are always welcome.

Linda Starke, Series Editor

Foreword

When contemplating this book, my thoughts went back
to the fall of 1965. The Agency for International Development (AID) Mission had asked the U.S. Department
of Agriculture for some help in evaluating an early draft
of India's next Five-Year Plan. Secretary of Agriculture
Orville Freeman decided that since I was working in the
Asia Analysis Branch in the Economic Research Service
and had lived in Indian villages in 1956, I would be the
one to go.

The goal for the 1965 harvest was 95 million tons of
grain, and this was the number the U.S. Embassy had
been using in its preliminary crop reports to Washington. Soon after arriving, I began to wonder whether anything even close to that would materialize. Reading several Indian newspapers each morning—the *Times of*

India, the *Hindu,* and the *Indian Express*—I found reports of drought in virtually every corner of the country.
Although some part of India is always experiencing a
drought, and there are floods somewhere every year, in
1965 the drought appeared to be everywhere.

Other bits and pieces of information made me dubi-
ous about the projected harvest. At a reception, I met
the director of Indian activities for Exxon (then called
Esso). When I asked him how business was, he said it
was great—irrigation fuel sales were nearly double the
previous year's because farmers were pumping day and
night to try and save their crops. Someone I had wanted
to meet in the Embassy, but who had planned on being
away on vacation, was actually there when I arrived. He
was a duck hunter, and usually took off a few weeks in
the fall to go hunting up north. But this year he can-
celled his vacation because the lake where he normally
hunted was dry. An agronomist working with AID and
attached to one of the state universities routinely
stopped his car to take soil samples when travelling the
several hundred miles between New Delhi and his university post. Analyzing these samples was a hobby. But
he complained to me that he could not get good core
samples with his auger: the soil was so dry, it crumbled
and fell out as he withdrew the auger.

After pondering these points and compiling information from newspaper reports on crop damage from various states and districts, I was convinced that India faced
a huge crop shortfall. I became sufficiently concerned
that I sent an urgent cable to Secretary Freeman in
Washington saying I didn't think there was any chance
India would harvest 95 million tons of grain, that they
probably would not harvest 80 million tons, and they
might not even harvest 70 million tons. With a deficit of

this scale a possibility in my mind at least, I felt Freeman needed this news as quickly as possible because it would take time to move wheat from the grain elevators in Kansas to our ports if an emergency food relief effort became necessary.

As I sent the cable, I had the strange feeling that I might be the only person who saw a crop shortfall of this magnitude. When the final data on the harvest were in some months later, it turned out to be some 77 million tons of grain, 18 million tons less than had been expected. In the effort to stave off famine that year, the United States shipped a fifth of its wheat harvest to India, some 10 million tons. At that time, it was the largest movement of food ever between two countries. Some 600 ships, nearly two a day, left U.S. ports for India laden with wheat. Measured by the number of ships used in a single operation, it ranked second only to the Allied crossing of the English Channel on D-Day. This record food assistance effort avoided what could have been one of the largest famines in history.

India had almost no food reserves to draw on to deal with this emergency. Indeed, when asked about the situation, a senior Indian government official replied, "Our reserves are in the grain elevators in Kansas." Indirectly, they had been led to depend on this because of a four-year food aid agreement arranged by President Eisenhower to supply them with 16 million tons of grain and a million tons of rice. This agreement, signed in 1959, effectively postponed any major resource commitments to agriculture by the Indian government.

As the food crisis unfolded in India, the extremely able Minister of Agriculture, C.S. Subramaniam, began to focus on long-term steps to improve the situation. Before long I was asked by Secretary Freeman to help draft an agricultural strategy for India that would give it greater food security. In retrospect, it was a rather easy assignment. We knew what India had to do. Its food price policy, which catered to urban dwellers by imposing ceiling prices on farm commodities, had to be reversed to provide floor prices for those growing the crops. If farmers were to invest in irrigation pumps, fertilizer, and land improvements, they had to know they could get a price for their wheat and rice that would at least cover their costs.

We knew that fertilizer supplies had to increase rapidly by shifting production to the private sector. Until that time, fertilizer plants were being built in the public sector. But it was taking an average of nine years to build one once the decision was made to do so, a laggardly performance that was leading to severe fertilizer shortages.

We also knew that the high-yielding dwarf varieties of wheat initially developed in Mexico had been tested in India and had performed very well. At that point, it seemed clear that India needed to accelerate the dissemination of these high-yielding seeds, varieties that would produce twice as much per unit of land and water as traditional varieties. To short-circuit the time-consuming process of multiplying seed in test plots over a number of years, we suggested that the Indian government import a couple of shiploads of wheat directly from Mexico in order to get seed to their farmers quickly.

These were some of the key steps in a highly successful agricultural development strategy—one that led to a doubling of India's wheat harvest in seven years, a record for a leading food staple in a major country. No country, not even the United States, had ever managed such rapid growth.

The encouraging thing about the situation in late 1965 was that we knew exactly what had to be done. There was no question. There was an enormous backlog of agricultural technology that could be brought to play in India to help eradicate hunger and stave off the threat of future famine. At that time, I noted that the new technologies would not solve the food problem. They would only buy time with which to slow population growth.

Unfortunately, the Indian government did not follow through with a successful grassroots-based family planning program. The result is that nearly three decades later, its total grain harvest has nearly doubled, but so has its population. With population climbing from 496 million to 915 million, its per capita grain production has risen only slightly.

The difference between then and now is that the nation is already using most of the technologies available to raise food production. If I were asked by the Indian government today to draft an agricultural strategy that would dramatically boost its food output in order to eliminate hunger, diversify diets, and provide for 590 million additional people over the next four decades, I could not do so. Nor do I know anyone who could.

There is still a substantial potential for expanding food output in India, but it consists of a little here and a little there rather than quantum jumps as in the past. Since 1965, India has more than doubled its irrigated area, but some of this has come at the cost of overpumping and aquifer depletion. Farmers can use more fertilizer, but the nation's use is already two thirds that of the United States. The big question for India and for scores of other countries is how to keep food production climbing rapidly without overpumping and overplowing.

As Hal Kane and I have been writing this book and

making projections of ballooning food deficits for many developing countries—deficits far larger than those projected officially by the U.N. Food and Agriculture Organization and the World Bank—I feel a bit like I did when drafting that cable in the fall of 1965. Now, as then, I hope this analysis will help draw attention to the new situation in time to do something about it.

Lester R. Brown

Full House

1

Entering a New Era

As the nineties unfold, the world is entering a new era, one in which it is far more difficult to expand food output. Many knew that this time would eventually come, that at some point the limits of the earth's natural systems, the cumulative effects of environmental degradation on cropland productivity, and the shrinking backlog of yield-raising technologies would slow the record growth in food production of recent decades. But because no one knew exactly when or how this would happen, the food prospect was widely debated. Now we can see that several constraints are emerging simultaneously to slow the growth in food production.

After nearly four decades of unprecedented expansion in both land-based and oceanic food supplies, the world is experiencing a massive loss of momentum. Between

1950 and 1984, world grain production expanded 2.6-fold, outstripping population growth by a wide margin and raising the grain harvested per person by 40 percent. Growth in the world fish catch was even more spectacular—a 4.6-fold increase between 1950 and 1989, which doubled seafood consumption per person. Together, these developments reduced hunger and malnutrition throughout the world, offering hope that these biblical scourges would one day be eliminated.[1]

But in recent years these trends suddenly have been reversed. After expanding at 3 percent a year from 1950 to 1984, the growth in grain production has slowed abruptly, rising at scarcely 1 percent annually from 1984 until 1993. As a result, grain production per person fell 12 percent during this time. (See Table 1–1.)[2]

With the fish catch, it is not merely a slowing of growth, but a limit imposed by nature. In 1989, the fish catch (including small contributions from inland catch and aquaculture) reached 100 million tons. After achieving this level, believed to be close to the maximum

TABLE 1-1. *World Production Per Person of Grain, Seafood, and Beef and Mutton, 1950–93*

Foodstuff	Trend Per Person			
	Growth Period	Growth	Decline Period	Decline
		(percent)		(percent)
Grain	1950–84	+ 40	1984–93	− 12
Seafood	1950–88	+ 126	1988–93	− 9
Beef and Mutton	1950–72	+ 36	1972–93	− 13

SOURCE: See endnote 2.

that oceanic fisheries can sustain, the catch has fluctuated between 96 million and 98 million tons. As a result, the 1993 per capita seafood catch was 9 percent below that of 1988. Marine biologists at the U.N. Food and Agriculture Organization (FAO) report that the 17 major oceanic fisheries are all now being fished at or beyond capacity and that 9 are in a state of decline.[3]

The world's rangelands, a major source of animal protein, are also under excessive pressure. The language used to describe them is similar to that used for fisheries: they are being grazed at or beyond capacity on every continent. This means that rangeland production of beef and mutton may not increase much, if at all, in the future. Here, too, availability per person will decline indefinitely as population grows.

With both fisheries and rangelands being pressed to the limits of their carrying capacity, future growth in food demand can be satisfied only by expanding output from croplands. The growth in demand for food that until recently was satisfied by three food systems must now all be satisfied by one.[4]

From mid-century until recently, grain output projections were for the most part simple extrapolations of trends. The past was a reliable guide to the future. But in a world of limits, this is changing. In projecting food supply trends now, at least six new constraints need to be taken into account:

► One, the backlog of unused agricultural technology is shrinking, leaving the more progressive farmers fewer agronomic options for expanding food output.
► Two, growing human demands are pressing against the limits of fisheries to supply seafood and of rangelands to supply beef, mutton, and milk.
► Three, demands for water are pressing against the

limits of the hydrological cycle to supply irrigation water in key food-growing regions.

▶ Four, in many countries, the use of additional fertilizer on currently available crop varieties has little or no effect on yields.

▶ Five, countries that are already densely populated when they begin to industrialize risk losing cropland at a rate that exceeds the rise in land productivity, initiating a long-term decline in food production.

▶ Six, social disintegration, often fed by rapid population growth and environmental degradation, is undermining many national governments and their efforts to expand food production.

First, in terms of agricultural technology, the contrast between mid-century and today could not be more striking. When the fifties began, a great deal of technology was waiting to be used. Except for irrigation, which goes back several thousand years, all the basic advances were made between 1840 and 1940. Justus von Liebig had discovered in 1847 that all the nutrients taken from the soil by crops could be replaced in mineral form. Gregor Mendel's work establishing the basic principles of heredity, which laid the groundwork for future crop breeding advances, was done in the 1860s. Hybrid corn varieties were commercialized in the United States during the twenties. And the dwarfing of wheat and rice plants in Japan to boost fertilizer responsiveness dates back a century.[5]

These long-standing technologies have been enhanced and modified for wide use through agricultural research and exploited by farmers during the last four decades. Although new technologies continue to appear, none promise to lead to quantum leaps in world food output. The relatively easy gains have been made. Moreover, public funding for international agricultural research has begun to decline. As a result, the more progressive farmers are looking over the shoulders of agricultural scientists seeking new yield-raising technologies—and discovering that they have less and less to offer. The pipeline has not run dry, but the flow has slowed to a trickle.[6]

In Asia, rice yields on maximum-yield experimental plots have not increased for more than two decades. Some countries appear to be "hitting the wall" as their yields approach those on the research plots. Japan reached this point with a rice yield in 1984 at 4.7 tons per hectare, a level it has been unable to top in nine harvests since then. South Korea, with similar growing conditions, may have run into the same barrier in 1988 when its rice yield stopped rising. Indonesia, whose rice yield has increased little since 1988, may be the first tropical rice-growing country to see its yield rise lose momentum. Other countries could hit the wall before the end of this decade.[7]

Farmers and policymakers search in vain for new advances, perhaps from biotechnology, that will lift world food output quickly to a new level. But biotechnology has not produced any yield-raising technologies that will lead to quantum jumps in output, nor do many researchers expect it to. Donald Duvick, for many years the director of research at the Iowa-based Pioneer Hi-Bred International, one of the world's largest seed suppliers, makes this point all too clearly: "No breakthroughs are in sight. Biotechnology, while essential to progress, will not produce sharp upward swings in yield potential except for isolated crops in certain situations."[8]

The productivity of oceanic fisheries and rangelands, both natural systems, is determined by nature. It can be reduced by overfishing and overgrazing or other forms of mismanagement, but once sustainable yield limits are reached, the contribution of these systems to world food supply cannot be expanded. As noted earlier, all oceanic fisheries are being pressed to their limits and beyond. And the decline in fisheries is not limited to developing countries: by early 1994, the United States was experiencing precipitous drops in fishery stocks off the coast of New England, off the West Coast, and in the Gulf of Mexico.[9]

With water—the third constraint—the overpumping that is now so widespread will eventually be curbed to bring it into balance with aquifer recharge. This reduction, combined with the growing diversion of irrigation water to residential and industrial uses, limits the amount of water available to produce food. Where farmers now depend on fossil aquifers for their irrigation water—in the southern U.S. Great Plains, for example, or the wheat fields of Saudi Arabia—aquifer depletion means an end to irrigated agriculture. In the United States, where more than a fourth of irrigated cropland is watered by drawing down underground water tables, the downward adjustment in irrigation pumping will be substantial. Major food-producing regions where overpumping is commonplace include the southern Great Plains, India's Punjab, and the North China Plain. For many of the world's farmers, the best hope for more water is from gains in efficiency.[10]

Perhaps the most worrisome emerging constraint on food production is the limited capacity of grain varieties to respond to the use of additional fertilizer. In the United States, Western Europe, and Japan, fertilizer use has increased little if at all during the last decade. Using additional amounts on existing crop varieties has little or no effect on yield in these countries. After a tenfold increase in world fertilizer use from 1950 to 1989—from 14 million to 146 million tons—use actually declined in the following four years.[11]

A little recognized threat to the future world food balance is the heavy loss of cropland that occurs when countries that are already densely populated begin to industrialize. The experience in Japan, South Korea, and Taiwan gives a sense of what to expect. The conversion of grainland to nonfarm uses and to high-value specialty crops has cost Japan 52 percent of its grainland, South Korea 42 percent, and Taiwan 35 percent.[12]

As the loss of land proceeded, it began to override the rise in land productivity, leading to declines in production. From its peak, Japan's grain production has dropped 33 percent, South Korea's has fallen 31 percent, and Taiwan's, 19 percent. These declines occurred at a time when population growth and rapidly rising incomes were driving up the demand for grain. The result is that by 1993 Japan was importing 77 percent of its grain, South Korea was bringing in 68 percent, and Taiwan, 74 percent.[13]

Asia's densely populated giants, China and India, are now going through the same stages that led to the extraordinarily heavy dependence on imported grain in the three smaller countries that industrialized earlier. In both, the shrinkage in grainland has begun. It is one thing for Japan, a country of 120 million people, to import 77 percent of its grain, but quite another if China, with 1.2 billion people, moves in this direction.

Further complicating efforts to achieve an acceptable balance between food and people is the social disinte-

gration occurring in many parts of the world. In a landmark article in the February 1994 *Atlantic* entitled "The
Coming Anarchy," writer and political analyst Robert
Kaplan observed that unprecedented population growth
and environmental degradation were driving people
from the countryside into cities and across national borders at a record rate. This, in turn, he reasoned, was
leading to social disintegration and political fragmentation. In parts of Africa, he argues, nation-states no longer exist in any meaningful sense. In their place are frag-
mented tribal and ethnic groups.[14]

The sequence of events that leads to environmental
degradation is all too familiar to environmentalists. It
begins when the firewood demands of a growing population exceed the sustainable yield of local forests, leading
to deforestation. As firewood becomes scarce, cow dung
and crop residues are burned for fuel, depriving the land
of nutrients and organic matter. Livestock numbers expand more or less apace with the human population,
eventually exceeding grazing capacity. The combination
of deforestation and overgrazing increase rainfall runoff
and soil erosion, simultaneously reducing aquifer recharge and soil fertility. No longer able to feed themselves, people become environmental refugees, heading
for the nearest city or food relief center.

Crop reports for African countries now regularly cite
weather and civil disorder as the key variables affecting
harvest prospects. Not only is agricultural progress difficult, under these circumstances even providing food aid
can be a challenge. In Somalia, getting food to the starving in late 1992 required a U.N. peacekeeping force and
military expenditures that probably cost 10 times as
much as the food that was distributed.

As political fragmentation and instability spread,

national governments can no longer provide the physical and economic infrastructure for development. Countries in this category include Afghanistan, Haiti, Liberia, Sierra Leone, and Somalia. To the extent that nation-states become dysfunctional, the prospects for humanely slowing population growth, for reversing environmental degradation, and for systematically expanding food production are diminished.[15]

The six limits or constraints briefly discussed here have emerged rather recently. In many cases, they were not anticipated. All available projections of world fertilizer use made during the eighties, for example, showed growth continuing smoothly through the remainder of the century and into the next. Few analysts anticipated the scale of water scarcity that is unfolding in large parts of the world. Many assumed that the agricultural research establishment could continue to churn out new technologies that would rapidly raise crop yields for the indefinite future. And few have even asked the question of what happens if China starts losing cropland as fast as Japan has during the last few decades.

Other negative influences, such as various forms of environmental degradation, also exist, but they have emerged more gradually. Among those that affect food production more directly are soil erosion, the waterlogging and salting of irrigated land, and air pollution. For example, a substantial share of the world's cropland is losing topsoil at a rate that exceeds natural soil formation. On newly cleared land that is steeply sloping, soil losses can lead to cropland abandonment in a matter of years. In other situations, the loss is slow and has a measurable effect on land productivity only over many decades.

Until recently, concerns about the earth's capacity to

feed ever growing numbers of people adequately was
confined largely to the environmental and population
communities and a few scientists. During the nineties,
however, these issues are arousing the concerns of the
mainstream scientific community. In early 1992, the
U.S. National Academy of Sciences and the Royal Society of London issued a report that began: "If current
predictions of population growth prove accurate and
patterns of human activity on the planet remain unchanged, science and technology may not be able to prevent either irreversible degradation of the environment
or continued poverty for much of the world."[16]

It was a remarkable statement, an admission that science and technology can no longer ensure a better future unless population growth slows quickly and the
economy is restructured. This abandonment of the
technological optimism that has permeated so much of
the twentieth century by two of the world's leading
scientific bodies represents a major shift—though perhaps not a surprising one, given the deteriorating state of
the planet. That they chose to issue a joint statement,
their first ever, reflects the deepening concern about the
future within the mainstream scientific community.

Later that same year, the Union of Concerned Scientists issued a "World Scientists Warning to Humanity"
signed by some 1,600 of the world's leading scientists,
including 102 Nobel Prize winners. It observes that the
continuation of destructive human activities "may so
alter the living world that it will be unable to sustain life
in the manner that we know." The scientists warned: "A
great change in our stewardship of the earth and the life
on it is required, if vast human misery is to be avoided
and our global home on this planet is not to be irretriev-
ably mutilated."[17]

And in November 1993, representatives of 56 national science academies convened in New Delhi, India, to discuss the population issue. At the end of their conference, they issued a statement in which they urged the world to move toward zero population growth during the lifetimes of their children.[18]

The time frame for projections of food and population in this book is the next four decades. It would be tempting to use a shorter period, but in dealing with basic policy questions—the need to stabilize both population and climate and to develop and disseminate new farming technologies—such an approach is of limited value. Data on food and population for the last four decades are included to provide both contrast and a historical perspective.

Between 1950 and 1990, for example, the world added 2.8 billion people, an average of 70 million a year. But between 1990 and 2030, the world is projected to add 3.6 billion, or 90 million a year. Even more troubling, nearly all this increase is projected for the developing countries, where life-support systems are already deteriorating. Such population growth in a finite ecosystem raises questions about the earth's carrying capacity. Will the earth's natural support systems sustain such growth indefinitely? How many people can the earth support at a given level of consumption?[19]

Underlying this assessment of population carrying capacity is the assumption that the food supply will be the most immediate constraint on population growth. Water scarcity could limit population growth in some locations, but it is unlikely to do so for the world as a whole in the foreseeable future. A buildup of environmental pollutants could interfere with human reproduction, much as DDT reduced the reproductive capacity

of bald eagles, peregrine falcons, and other birds at the
top of the food chain. In the extreme, accumulating pollutants in the environment could boost death rates to
the point where they would exceed birth rates, leading to
a gradual decline in human numbers, but this does not
seem likely. For now, it appears that the food supply will
be the most immediate, and therefore the controlling,
determinant of how many people the earth can support.

Full House reassesses the earth's population carrying
capacity as measured by food output, taking into account the constraints just discussed. Grain supply and
demand projections are undertaken to 2030 for the 13
most populous countries (see Chapters 12 and 13), a
group that accounts for two thirds of world population
and food production. These incorporate the latest information on the emerging constraints on production, and
they show much slower growth in output than the official projections by the Food and Agriculture Organization and the World Bank.[20]

If the FAO and World Bank projections of relative
abundance and a continuing decline of food prices materialize, then governments can get by with business as
usual. If, on the other hand, the constraints incorporated into the *Full House* projections are reasonable,
then the world needs to fundamentally reorder priorities, recognizing that food scarcity has replaced military
aggression as the principal threat to our security. If our
projections are at all close to the mark, family planners
will have to assume much of the responsibility for establishing a more humane balance between food and people.

The principal underlying difference is that the FAO
and World Bank studies assume grain yield per hectare
will continue to rise at more or less the same rate during

the next two decades as it did in the last three. A second difference is that the other studies only project to 2010, whereas the projections in *Full House* go to 2030, giving the disparity between continuing rapid population growth and the finite capacities of the earth's natural systems much more time to unfold. And third, the two official studies fail to recognize the potential heavy loss of cropland to nonfarm uses in China and the associated decline in production, a drop that greatly affects the global grain balance.

At the national level, the projections in *Full House* provide some sense of likely food production gains over the longer term. As governments refine these carrying capacity assessments in much more detail than is possible here, they can share the resulting information on expected food supplies with people, initiating a national discussion of what combination of population size and food consumption levels is desirable.

At the international level, our projections suggest that the population-driven environmental deterioration/political disintegration scenario described by Robert Kaplan is not only possible; indeed, it is likely in a business-as-usual world. But it is not inevitable. This future can be averted if security is redefined, recognizing that food scarcity, not military aggression, is the principal threat to our future. This would lead to a massive reordering of priorities—giving top place to filling the family planning gap; to attacking the underlying causes of high fertility, such as illiteracy and poverty; to protecting soil and water resources; and to raising investment in agriculture.

I

Reading the Trends

2

Food Insecurity

Recent decades have witnessed record gains in food production. Even Africa has more than doubled its grain harvest. Nonetheless, an estimated 900 million people are hungry, many of them getting only one meal a day. For many in this group, making it to the next harvest is an annual challenge. For them, food security is the focus of their existence, the key to their survival.[1]

There are many measures of food security, from the personal to the global. The two most useful global indicators are grain production per person and carryover stocks of grain. The first gives a sense of whether overall food availability is improving or deteriorating; the second shows if production is exceeding consumption or if the opposite is occurring. Both are physical indicators, easy to measure and compare over time and from country to country.

Grain is a useful measure of food security for two reasons. One, consumed directly it supplies half of human food energy intake, and it provides part of the remainder indirectly in the form of meat, milk, eggs, cheese, and butter. Two, because it is less perishable than fruits and vegetables, grain can be stored to supply food during the winter season in the higher latitudes and during the dry season in areas with monsoonal climates.

World grain production increased from 631 million tons in 1950 to 1,649 million tons in 1984, a 2.6-fold increase. The period was a remarkable one for the world's farmers: in 34 years they doubled the harvest once and started to double it again. Then growth in output began to lose momentum as the yield response to additional fertilizer fell sharply. From 1950 to 1984, grain output expanded at 3 percent annually, but during the following nine years it grew less than 1 percent a year.[2]

The trend of grain production per person is more revealing. From 1950 until 1984 it climbed from 247 kilograms to 346, a rise of 40 percent. Hunger was retreating in scores of countries. But during the next nine years, per capita production fell by more than one tenth to 303 kilograms. (See Figure 2–1.)[3]

Although these numbers show the global trend, they do not reflect the contrasting developments within regions. In Western Europe, for example, grain output per person climbed dramatically as high support prices stimulated the adoption of advanced agricultural technologies while population growth was coming to a halt. In Africa, in contrast, the farming technologies that could be applied in semiarid regions were limited and population growth was the fastest of any continent in history, leading to a steady decline. Similarly, India's

Kilograms

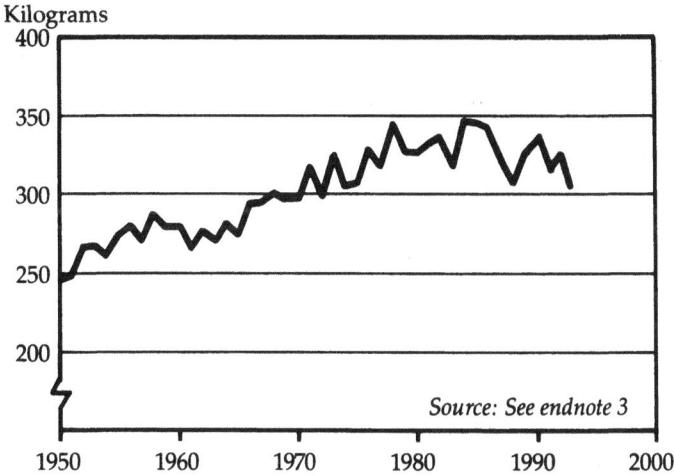

FIGURE 2-1. *World Grain Production Per Person, 1950–93*

grain production per person today has risen only one fifth since the Green Revolution began 30 years ago, while China's has increased by close to half since the agricultural reforms of 1978, giving it substantial amounts of grain for conversion into livestock products.[4]

World carryover stocks of grain—the amount in the bin when the new harvest begins—are a second key indicator of food security for the world's 5.5 billion people. When stocks drop below 60 days of consumption, there is scarcely enough to keep supply lines operating. In the modern world, where consumers and producers are widely separated, large quantities of grain are required just to keep the pipeline between the two filled. Wheat moving from U.S. farms to Russian consumers, for instance, passes through a grain elevator near a wheat farm in the Great Plains, a train, a portside elevator, a ship, a portside elevator in Russia, a train to an elevator at a flour mill, and a truck to a bakery; bread is then finally distributed in the community where it will be eaten. An interruption anywhere along this supply line can disrupt consumption.[5]

During the 30 years for which data are available, world grain stocks have ranged from a low of 159 million tons in 1966 to a high of 465 million tons in 1987. The more meaningful measure, however, is how many days of use these stocks represent. As world consumption has doubled, the amount needed to provide an equivalent amount of security has also doubled. The highest level of stocks ever held was in 1987, at 104 days of world grain consumption. (See Figure 2–2.) The lowest was the 55 days in 1973, an amount that caused grain prices to more than double.[6]

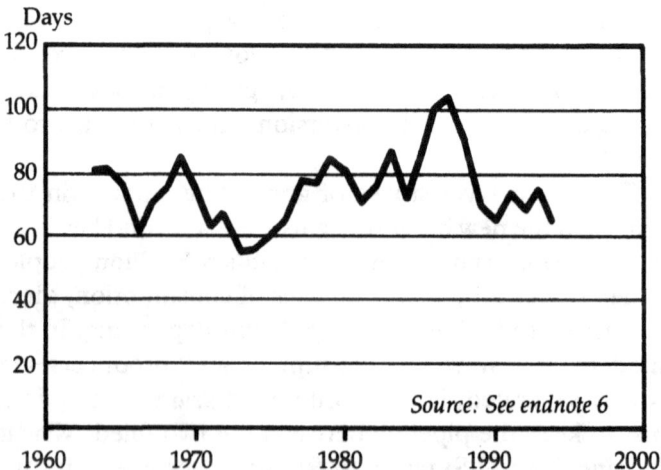

FIGURE 2-2. *World Grain Carryover Stocks as Days of Consumption, 1963–94*

Whenever stocks are falling and approach 60 days of consumption, grain markets become quite nervous. An adverse weather report from any major food-producing region in the world can trigger a dramatic price rise. With 1994 carryover stocks down to 62 days of consumption, grain prices have been uncommonly volatile. In late 1993, when it became clear that rice carryover stocks in 1994 would fall to the lowest level in 20 years, partly because of a poor harvest in Japan, rice prices doubled between the end of August and mid-November.[7]

In 1991, 1992, and 1993, world rice consumption exceeded production. The key question in 1994 is whether the rice growers of Asia, who produce more than 90 percent of the world crop, can catch up with the growth in demand and then overtake it to rebuild stocks. If they cannot, then high rice prices could join high seafood prices as part of the economic landscape.

In addition to carryover stocks, the world has a second line of defense against food shortages—the cropland idled under U.S. commodity programs and, more recently, programs in Europe, though the latter area is small. In the early seventies, when world grain prices doubled, the 23.8 million hectares held out of production under U.S. commodity programs in 1972 was largely released for use in 1973. When farmers still found it difficult to rebuild world stocks, the remainder was released for cultivation in 1974. For the next decade little or no U.S. land was held out of cultivation. In 1994, the United States once again released for cultivation all cropland in commodity set-aside programs except for 2 million hectares of cotton land, in an effort to rebuild stocks.[8]

An additional 14 million hectares of highly erodible

U.S. cropland has been planted to grass or trees since early 1986 under the Conservation Reserve Program. This land has been set aside for conservation under 10-year contracts with the U.S. Department of Agriculture (USDA). The first of these begin to expire in late 1995. Of the 14 million hectares, part could be farmed sustainably if soil-conserving agricultural practices were adopted, such as the rotation of row crops with forage crops or the use of minimum tillage practices.[9]

A third reserve is the grain fed to livestock and poultry, an amount in excess of 600 million tons yearly, roughly one third of the harvest. Although all grains fed to livestock can be consumed as food, this reserve is far more difficult to tap. A substantial rise in world grain prices would reduce the amount fed to livestock, but it would also lower the direct consumption of grain among the world's poorest people, perhaps even threatening their survival.[10]

Aside from the depletion of world grain stocks, the overwhelming dependence on North America—where agricultural output in both the United States and Canada is affected by the same climatic cycle—introduces a special dimension of food insecurity. A drought in the United States is invariably accompanied by one in Canada. In 1988, when the U.S. grain harvest was reduced 27 percent by record heat and drought, that of Canada was down by 31 percent. With these two countries controlling a larger share of grain exports than the Middle East does of oil, weather conditions are of concern to food-importing countries everywhere.[11]

The risk in depending heavily on North America is evident. At the time of the severe drought in 1988, world grain stocks—mostly in the United States—were at a near record level. If another such drought were to occur in North America with world food stocks at the low level of the mid-nineties, world grain prices would go off the top of the chart, creating a world food emergency.

Another source of food insecurity is the growing share of the world grain harvest that is produced with the unsustainable use of land and water. When world food supplies tightened in the early seventies and grain prices doubled, farmers responded with some impressive gains in output, but part of the gains came from overplowing and overpumping. Plowing highly erodible land caused heavy soil losses, and overpumping underground water for irrigation lowered water tables.[12]

By definition, farmers can overplow and overpump only in the short run. For some, the short run is drawing to a close. This is leading to agricultural retrenchment as farmers pull back from the excesses of the past. No one knows how much of the world's food output is unsustainable, but the situation in the United States provides some examples. As noted earlier, the United States has converted 11 percent of its cropland to grassland or woodland because it was too erodible to sustain continuous cropping. And USDA reports that water tables are falling by 6 inches to 4 feet per year beneath one fourth of U.S. irrigated cropland, indicating that eventual pumping cutbacks are inevitable.[13]

If the U.S. grain output that is produced unsustainably is subtracted from total world output, the market surpluses of the last decade or so disappear. If enough data were available on soil erosion and falling water tables in other countries to extend this calculation worldwide, it would undoubtedly show sustainable world food output running well below consumption.

Another source of unfounded optimism in recent years has been the output stimulated by high government farm price supports, which are typically well above world market levels, and the fertilizer and irrigation subsidies that bring the price to farmers well below the market level. Fiscal stringencies in the early nineties coupled with economic reforms in some countries, including the former Soviet Union and Eastern Europe, have reduced many of these subsidies. Negotiations under the General Agreement on Tariffs and Trade—also intended to lower support prices and thereby expand agricultural markets for exporting countries—are expected to have a similar effect.

For nearly four decades, food aid has provided security to those threatened with harvest failures. The United States, for example, shipped one fifth of its wheat crop to India two years in a row during the sixties after back-to-back monsoon failures. At roughly 10 million tons of grain per year, the volume of food aid has remained remarkably stable for three decades. But the program has shifted from just offsetting poor harvests to also providing food relief to countries, such as Ethiopia, that are chronically short of food and lack the foreign exchange to buy it. Given the growing deficits in many such countries, particularly in Africa, there will be a need for even more concessional assistance at a time when food aid programs, caught in a downward spiral of foreign aid funding, may not expand much, if at all.[14]

Aside from physical indicators of food security, such as grain production per person and carryover stocks, two economic indicators—food prices and personal incomes—are of particular interest to policymakers. Since mid-century, real prices of the world's two principal food staples, wheat and rice, have declined dramatically, reflecting widespread gains in production efficiency. The price of wheat, for example, which averaged over

$200 a ton in the fifties, is scarcely $100 a ton today (1985 dollars). Similarly, rice prices, at some $500 a ton in the fifties, had fallen to $200 per ton by the early nineties. These unprecedented drops in real food prices during the last four decades have contributed broadly to improving diets, particularly among those with low incomes. (See Figure 2–3.)[15]

As grain prices fell from mid-century onward, personal incomes were rising almost everywhere during the century's third quarter. Then the rise in incomes began to slow. During the eighties, incomes fell in some 49 countries, home to 846 million people. Almost all were low-income, largely agrarian economies where rapid population growth, environmental degradation, and deepening poverty are reinforcing each other in a downward spiral. One consequence of this is a widening of the

Dollars
Per Ton

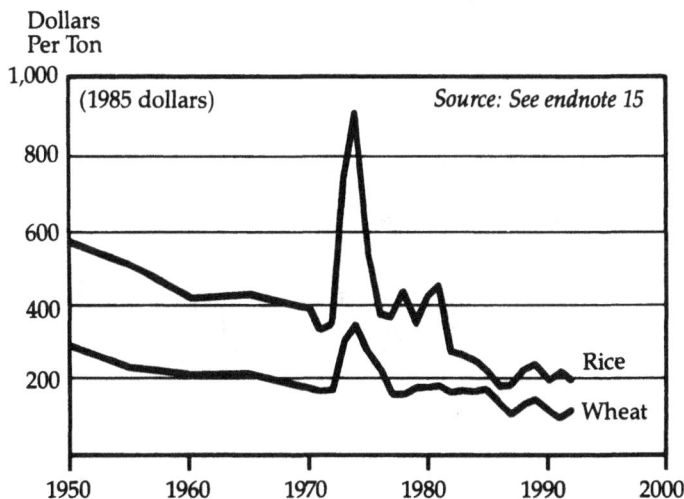

FIGURE 2-3. *Wheat and Rice Prices, 1950–93*

income gap between the richest and the poorest. In 1960, the ratio of the richest 20 percent of the world to the poorest 20 percent was 30 to 1. In each decade since then, the gap has widened, reaching 64 to 1 in 1990. (See Table 2–1.)[16]

The risk is that slower growth of the world economy will close the door on many with low incomes. After reaching its historical high of 5.2 percent a year during the sixties, the economy slowed some in the seventies and still further in the eighties, dropping to 2.9 percent. (See Table 2–2.) Despite this, the average per capita output of goods and services rose as overall economic growth stayed ahead of population. Now that, too, may be changing.[17]

From 1990 to 1993, the world economy expanded annually at just 0.9 percent, leading to a per capita decline of 0.8 percent a year. Thus three years into the new decade, income per person was already 2 percent lower than it was when the nineties began. Even using an economic accounting system that overstates progress because it omits the depletion of natural capital, living standards have fallen.[18]

TABLE 2–1. *Global Income Distribution, 1960–90*

Year	Share of Global Income Going to Richest 20 Percent	Share of Global Income Going to Poorest 20 Percent	Ratio of Richest to Poorest
	(percent)		
1960	70.2	2.3	30 to 1
1970	73.9	2.3	32 to 1
1980	76.3	1.7	45 to 1
1990	82.8	1.3	64 to 1

SOURCE: See endnote 16.

TABLE 2-2. *World Economic Growth by Decade, Total and Per Capita, 1950–93*

Decade	Annual Growth	Annual Growth Per Person
	(percent)	
1950–60	4.9	3.1
1960–70	5.2	3.2
1970–80	3.4	1.6
1980–90	2.9	1.1
1990–93 (prel.)	0.9	− 0.8

SOURCE: See endnote 17.

As incomes among the poor fall, the nature of famine itself is changing. Traditionally it was geographically defined, concentrated where there were crop failures. With today's worldwide food distribution system, malnutrition so severe that it is life-threatening is found mainly among the Third World's landless rural laborers and urban poor. Although the hungry are more dispersed and less visible, they are no less numerous. A recent U.N. Development Programme assessment puts the number of malnourished at some 900 million, one in six persons.[19]

The deteriorating economic position of the poorest one fifth of humanity, who spend most of their income on food, combined with the collapse in purchasing power in the former Soviet Union help explain why grain prices have not risen in recent years, even though grain production per person has been falling.[20]

Given the emerging constraints in growth in output, the long decline in real food prices may have come to an end. Seafood prices are already rising as the demand for seafood increases while the catch remains static. After seafood, the price of rice could be the next to rise, simply because production is restricted by the scarcity not only of cropland but also of fresh water.

When the world rice price doubled in the fall of 1993, it was bad news for consumers in low-income, rice-importing countries. For people already spending 70 percent of their income on food, a doubling in the rice price forced them to tighten their belts when there were no notches left.[21]

In sum, the world faces so many different sources of food insecurity in the mid-nineties—low carryover stocks of grain, less land idled under commodity programs, unsustainable use of land and water, and the cumulative effects of soil erosion and other forms of environmental degradation—that any major disruption, such as a severe drought in the United States or a monsoon failure in India, could trigger dramatic price rises. These in turn could undermine political stability simultaneously in scores of low-income grain-importing countries.

3

Ninety Million More

Everyone born before 1950 has witnessed a doubling of
world population, the first generation ever to do so. This
unprecedented growth is destroying agriculture's environmental support systems at record rates, reducing the
living standards of hundreds of millions. Mounting population pressures are driving growing numbers of people
from the countryside into the city and across national
boundaries, exacerbating ethnic, religious, and tribal
conflicts within societies.[1]

The effect of population growth is changing. At one
time, it merely slowed progress. Now in more and more
situations, it is reversing it. Stated otherwise, the demands of the 90 million people added each year for
grain and seafood are being satisfied by reducing consumption among those already here. This is a new situa-

tion, one that puts population policy in a new light.

Few people understand how explosive the prevailing population rates in recent decades can be. A population that expands by 3 percent in one year may not seem to pose much of a threat. But compounded over decades, it can devastate local life-support systems.

In 1975, the senior author received a letter addressing this point from Julius Nyrere, President of Tanzania. He wrote, "you say that 'not two in a hundred of national political leaders knows that a population which increases by 3% a year will increase 19 times in a century', and you may well have been right. But whatever the number who had that knowledge, you have now increased it by a least one!"[2]

President Nyrere was commenting on *By Bread Alone*, which had pointed out that with a 3-percent growth rate, a country such as Algeria with just over 15 million people would see its population expand to 288 million within a century. He went on to say in his letter, "Your example on page 180 struck me very forcibly because the Algerian population of 15 million which you gave as your example is very roughly the same as the present Tanzanian population. That our population may be 288 million in a hundred years makes you (me!) think."[3]

Rapid population growth is so recent that we have difficulty both grasping its dimensions and understanding its effects. We struggle to describe what the annual addition of 90 million people means. Sometimes we express it in terms of countries: in effect, last year the world added the population equivalent of the United Kingdom, Belgium, Denmark, Sweden, and Norway combined. Sometimes we talk in terms of cities: each month the world adds another New York City.[4]

In late 1992, we watched the evening television news

with horror as thousands of Somalis died of starvation. During six months, an estimated 300,000 starved to death—a figure that is only comprehensible to most of us in terms of seeing 100,000 people in a sports stadium. It was a grievous loss, one that led to calls for U.N. military intervention to ensure that food aid could reach the starving in the midst of warring tribal factions. Yet massive though the loss of life was, it took the world only 29 hours to add a number equally large. Ninety million additional people a year, spread over 365 days, comes to a quarter-million a day—just over 10,000 an hour.[5]

The annual growth in world population is the result of an excess of births, roughly 140 million, over deaths of some 50 million. Of the 90 million added each year, 84 million live in the Third World. India is the principal contributor, adding 18 million compared with China's 15 million. In Africa, each of the three most populous countries—Egypt, Ethiopia, and Nigeria—adds more people than does all of Western Europe combined. In the western hemisphere, Brazil, adding nearly 3 million, exceeds the U.S. natural increase of just over 2 million.[6]

The fastest-growing regions are Africa and the Middle East, each expanding at almost 3 percent a year, and each with a particular set of population-related issues. In Africa, with the fastest population growth of any continent in history, per capita grain production has fallen nearly 20 percent since 1970, forcing the continent to import heavily. After a generation of unprecedented population growth in the strife-ridden Middle East, severe water shortages are emerging, raising the prospect that water could rival religion as a source of conflict within the region.[7]

At the other end of the spectrum, population growth in Europe stands at roughly 0.3 percent a year, bringing the region close to population stability. As of 1993, some 25 countries have essentially stable populations, where growth is between + 0.3 and -0.3 percent. (See Table 3–1.) Of this group, all except Japan are in

TABLE 3-1. *Countries With Essentially Stable Population Size, 1993*

Country	Natural Increase	Population
	(percent)	(million)
Austria	+ 0.2	8
Belarus	+ 0.2	10
Belgium	+ 0.2	10
Bulgaria	− 0.2	9
Croatia	+ 0.1	5
Czech Republic	+ 0.1	16
Denmark	+ 0.1	5
Estonia	0	2
Finland	+ 0.3	5
Germany	− 0.1	81
Greece	+ 0.1	10
Hungary	− 0.2	10
Italy	0	58
Japan	+ 0.3	124
Latvia	− 0.2	3
Luxembourg	+ 0.3	0.4
Portugal	+ 0.1	10
Romania	+ 0.1	23
Russia	+ 0.1	149
Slovenia	+ 0.3	2
Spain	+ 0.1	39
Sweden	+ 0.3	9
Switzerland	+ 0.3	7
Ukraine	− 0.1	52
United Kingdom	+ 0.3	60
Total		707

SOURCE: See endnote 8.

Europe. The largest, Russia, has 149 million people. The smallest, Luxembourg, has only 400,000. These 25 countries—including three leading European industrial societies, Germany, Italy, and the United Kingdom— contain more than 700 million people, 13 percent of the world total. Achieving an environmentally sustainable future depends on the rest of the world following in their footsteps.[8]

The annual addition to world population has increased from 38 million at mid-century to nearly 90 million in the mid-nineties. (See Figure 3–1.) Drops in the annual additions to world population in 1960, 1961, and 1962 were the result of massive famine in China. The disruption that followed the ill-conceived "Great Leap Forward" in 1958 led to a precipitous fall in food production. With the government unwilling to turn to

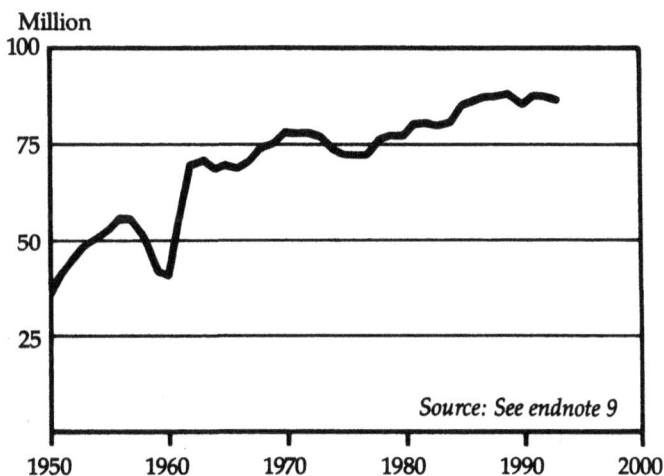

FIGURE 3-1. *Annual Addition to World Population, 1950–93*

the outside world for help, an estimated 30 million Chinese starved to death during the next few years. The increase in deaths, combined with a hunger-induced drop in births in China, was so extensive that it markedly slowed world population growth for a while.[9]

During the first half of the seventies, the number added gradually declined, from 78 million in 1970 to 73 million in 1975, largely as a result of reductions in family size in both China and India. Unfortunately, this trend did not continue. Shiro Horiuchi of Rockefeller University, in an analysis of fertility trends, showed that the decline in fertility in both China and India had stalled by 1980. In addition, the age structure of the world's population, particularly in developing countries, was dominated by young people entering their reproductive years. A third factor cited by Horiuchi was the lack of any new national fertility declines in the eighties. As a result, the number of annual additions resumed their longer term upward trend.[10]

Contributing to this loss of momentum in efforts to slow population growth was the U.S. withdrawal of funding from both the International Planned Parenthood Federation and the U.N. Population Fund. Combined with abnegation of U.S. leadership on the population issue, it led to a broad-based loss of momentum on the family planning front.[11]

Falling living standards in many poor countries were also a factor. In 1945, the eminent demographer Frank Notestein outlined a theory of demographic change based on the effect of economic and social progress on population growth. His theory, known as the demographic transition, classified all societies into one of three stages. Drawing heavily on the European experience, it has provided a useful conceptual framework for demographic research ever since.[12]

During the first stage of the demographic transition, which characterizes premodern societies, both birth and death rates are high and population grows slowly, if at all. In the second stage, living conditions improve as public health measures, including mass immunizations, are introduced and food production expands. Birth rates remain high, but death rates fall and population grows rapidly. The third stage follows when economic and social gains, combined with lower infant mortality rates, reduce the desire for large families. As in the first stage, birth rates and death rates are in equilibrium, but at a much lower level.[13]

This remarkably useful conceptualization has been widely used by demographers to explain differential rates of growth and to project future trends. But as we approach the end of the twentieth century, a gap has emerged in the analysis. The theorists did not say what happens when second-stage population growth rates of 3 percent per year begin to overwhelm local life-support systems, making it impossible to sustain the economic and social gains that are counted on to reduce births.

Unfortunately, trends that lead to ecological deterioration and economic decline are also self-reinforcing: Once populations expand to the point where their demands begin to exceed the sustainable yields of local forests, grasslands, croplands, or aquifers, they begin directly or indirectly to consume the resource base itself. Forests and grasslands disappear, soils erode, land productivity declines, water tables fall, and wells go dry. This, in turn, reduces food production and incomes, triggering a downward spiral in a process we describe as the demographic trap.

All countries either will complete the demographic transition, reaching population stability with low death and birth rates, or will get caught in the demographic trap, which eventually also will lead to demographic stability—but with high birth rates and high death rates. Close to half the world's people today live in countries that are now in their fifth decade of rapid population growth.

The risk in these countries is that death rates will begin to rise in response to declining living standards, pushing countries back into the first stage. In 1963, Frank Notestein, Dudley Kirk, and Sheldon Segal pointed out that "such a rise in mortality would demonstrate the bankruptcy of all our [development] efforts." For a number of countries, that specter of bankruptcy is growing uncomfortably close.[14]

The effect of varying rates of population growth on efforts to raise living standards can be seen in the trends in per capita grain production for Western Europe, the region with the slowest population growth since midcentury, and Africa, the region with the fastest. From 1950 to 1993, both regions more than doubled their grain production. Europe's output increased by 152 percent; Africa's by 118 percent. (See Figure 3–2.)[15]

Although their agricultural performances were similar, the per capita effects contrasted sharply. While Europe's output per person was doubling, going from 235 kilograms to nearly 500, Africa's dropped from 162 kilograms to 118, converting the continent into a grain importer and leaving millions of Africans hungry and physically weakened, drained of their vitality and productivity. Widely varying population growth rates account for the difference: In 1950, Western Europe actually had more people than Africa. But by 1993 Africa had nearly twice as many people as Western Europe.[16]

As noted earlier, the framework of analysis used in *Full House* compares the next four decades with the last

Kilograms

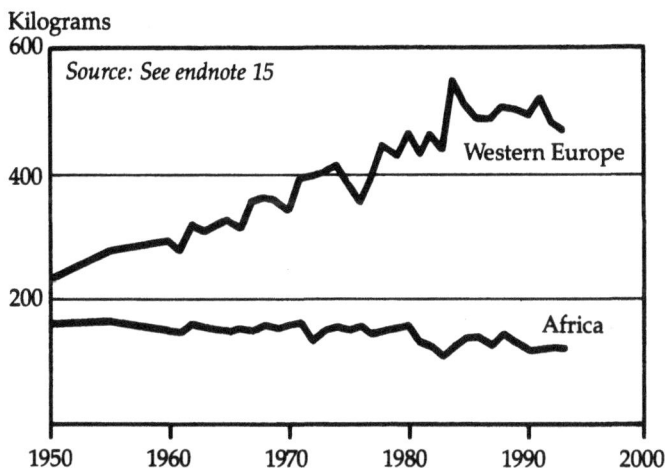

FIGURE 3-2. *Grain Production Per Person, Western Europe and Africa, 1950–93*

four. Table 3–2 shows world population in 1950 at 2.5 billion, increasing to 5.3 billion in 1990, for an addition of 2.8 billion. Between 1990 and 2030, the projection shows population rising to 8.9 billion, an addition of 3.6 billion. On an annual basis, this translates into an average increase from 1990 to 2030 of 90 million per year, compared with 70 million a year for the last four decades.[17]

The extent of the demographic divide in the world today can be seen rather clearly in Table 3–3. The 18 countries listed include all the more populous nations and account for two thirds of the world's population. Except for the United States, population growth in the more populous industrial countries has essentially stabilized, with no significant change in prospect during the next four decades. For the United States, a birth rate

TABLE 3-2. *World Population Growth, 1950–90, With Projections to 2030*

Year	Population	Population Growth	Population Growth Per Year
	(billion)	(billion)	(million)
1950	2.5		
1990	5.3	2.8	70
2030	8.9	3.6	90

SOURCE: See endnote 17.

of 16 per thousand and a death rate of 9 yields a current annual natural increase of 0.7 percent. This, coupled with a substantial immigration, leads to a projected growth of 95 million by 2030, roughly the same as during the last four decades.[18]

For developing countries, the situation is far different in comparison both with industrial countries and with the recent past. Nigeria, for example, which gained 55 million people from 1950 to 1990, is projected to add 191 million people during the next four decades. Ethiopia, which can no longer feed itself even when rainfall is good, is projected to add 106 million people by 2030—more three times as many as during the last 40 years. Iran faces increases of a similar magnitude. Pakistan will add nearly three times as many in the next four decades as during the last four. Bangladesh and Egypt will each add almost twice as many people. The largest absolute increase is slated for India: 590 million, compared with China at 490 million.[19]

To understand the staggering dimensions of the population growth facing a country like India, it is useful to juxtapose the projected gains with those for the United

TABLE 3-3. *Population Growth, 1950–90, With Projections to 2030, for the Most Populous Countries*[1]

Country	1950	1990	2030	Increase 1950–90	1990–2030
			(million)		
Slowly Growing Countries					
France	42	57	62	15	5
Germany	68	80	81	12	1
Italy	47	58	56	11	−2
Japan	84	124	123	40	−1
Russia	114	148	161	34	13
United King.	50	58	60	8	2
United States	152	250	345	98	95
Rapidly Growing Countries					
Bangladesh	46	114	243	68	129
Brazil	53	153	252	100	99
China	563	1,134	1,624	571	490
Egypt	21	54	111	33	57
Ethiopia & Erit.	21	51	157	30	106
India	369	853	1,443	484	590
Indonesia	83	189	307	106	118
Iran	16	57	183	41	126
Mexico	28	85	150	57	65
Nigeria	32	87	278	55	191
Pakistan	39	115	312	76	197

[1]Census Bureau data are used because they are updated more often than the U.N. medium-range projections; the two series are essentially the same.

SOURCE: See endnote 18.

States. Of the two, the United States has far more natural resources and capital for investment, and is overall much better equipped to deal with large population increases. But it is difficult to see how even the United States could cope with 590 million more people in the next 40 years without suffering a pronounced decline in living standards.

These massive increases projected for so many countries in the developing world (including many smaller ones not in Table 3–3) are the result either of nonexistent or failed population policies. As noted earlier, during the seventies world population growth showed signs of easing off, but efforts to slow growth then lost momentum, and in the mid-eighties the annual addition climbed sharply.[20]

As populations grow, the effect of population growth changes. Demographers and economists often focus on the rate of current and projected growth of population. If they are concerned about population growth and see that the rate of growth is declining, they are likely to feel satisfied. Biologists, however, distinguish between rate of growth and absolute size. They are concerned with the relationship between the demand of a given population and its support systems. Once the local demand for water rises above the rate of aquifer recharge, for example, any further growth—however slow—will deplete the aquifer, leading to severe water shortages. Similarly with firewood: once the demands of a village begin to exceed the regenerative capacity of local forests, they begin to disappear, gradually receding into the distance.

Local overruns of life-support systems are not new, but for the first time, growing human demand is crossing the sustainability threshold of global ecosystems. As discussed in Chapter 2, world demand for seafood has surpassed the sustainable yield of oceanic fisheries, challenging management skills at the international level. The same is true of livestock products from rangelands. It now seems certain that the deteriorating relationship between us and our natural support systems, and the economic effects of that changing relationship, will become a consuming concern of governments in the decades ahead.

4

Climbing the Food Chain

When asked by a *New York Times* reporter if living conditions were improving, a Chinese villager responded, "Overall life has gotten much better. My family eats meat maybe four or five times a week now. Ten years ago we never had meat." For this villager, like many others, progress is measured in meat consumption, in relieving the monotony of a diet consisting almost entirely of starches.[1]

In low-income countries, where diets are typically dominated by a single starchy staple, rises in income quickly translate into consumption of more livestock products and more fruits and vegetables. Consumption of more of either is a luxury the poor cannot afford. Just as converting grain into meat, milk, and eggs is inefficient, so, too, is the use of land to produce fruits and vegetables, such as lettuce, strawberries, and asparagus, simply because the yields of calories and protein per hectare are so much lower than with grain.

Among the world's affluent, it is the consumption of livestock products that claims a disproportionately large share of land and water resources. In low-income countries, grain consumption per person averages some 200 kilograms a year, roughly one pound a day. Diets are high in starch and low in fat and protein, with up to 70 percent or more of caloric intake coming from one staple, such as rice. By contrast, those living in affluent societies such as the United States and Canada, who are on the upper rungs of the grain consumption ladder, easily consume 800 kilograms of grain a year, most of it indirectly in the form of beef, mutton, pork, poultry, milk, cheese, yogurt, ice cream, and eggs. Thus the grain-consumption ratio between those living in the world's wealthiest and poorest countries is roughly four to one. Wide though this is, it is much less than for such items as energy consumption or health care expenditures, where it can exceed 30 to 1.[2]

The 800 kilograms of grain consumed per person each year in the United States translates into a diet rich in livestock products: as meat, it includes 42 kilograms of beef, 28 kilograms of pork, and 44 kilograms of poultry. (See Table 4–1.) From dairy cows, it includes 271 kilograms of milk, part of it consumed directly and part as cheese (12 kilograms), yogurt (2 kilograms), and ice cream (8 kilograms). Rounding out this protein-rich fare are more than 200 eggs a year.[3]

This contrasts sharply with the situation in India, where most of the 200 kilograms of grain available per person is eaten directly just to meet basic food energy needs. With little grain available to feed livestock and

TABLE 4-1. *Annual Per Capita Grain Use and Consumption of Livestock Products in Selected Countries, 1990*

Country	Grain Use[1]	Consumption					
		Beef	Pork	Poultry	Mutton	Milk[2]	Eggs
		(kilograms)					
United States	800	42	28	44	1	271	16
Italy	400	16	20	19	1	182	12
China	300	1	21	3	1	4	7
India	200	—	0.4	0.4	0.2	31	13

[1]Rounded to nearest 100 kilograms since the purpose of this table is to contrast the wide variations in consumption of livestock products for different categories of grain use. [2]Total consumption, including that used to produce cheese, yogurt, and ice cream.

SOURCE: See endnote 3.

poultry and with a limited cultural acceptance of beef, consumption of livestock products is low. For the average Indian, it totals 31 kilograms of milk; 1 kilogram of pork, poultry, and mutton combined; and about 170 eggs. Only in the consumption of eggs is India in the same category as industrial countries.[4]

In between the United States and India are Italy, using 400 kilograms of grain per person annually, and China, with 300 kilograms. The big difference between the United States and Italy is meat consumption: 115 kilograms per year versus 56. And just as India matches industrial countries in egg consumption per person, China nearly equals them in consumption of pork, its most popular livestock product. Among these four countries, life expectancy is highest in Italy—perhaps in part because it may have the healthiest all-around diet, one where animal protein intake is high enough that even the poor are adequately nourished but not so rich in animal fats that it damages health.[5]

World meat production in 1993, at an estimated 179 million tons, is up nearly fourfold from the 46 million tons produced in 1950. Few global economic trends have been as predictable as the growth in meat production over the past four decades. During most of this period, it expanded faster than population, raising the per capita production of meat from 18 kilograms in 1950 to 32 kilograms in 1987. Since then, it has slowed, increasing at roughly the same rate as population. As a result, the growth in per capita meat consumption has come to a halt, remaining at 32 kilograms for six years. (See Figure 4–1.)[6]

Throughout this period, the production of beef and pork have dominated. From 1950 into the late seventies, beef and pork production trends moved upward in lock-

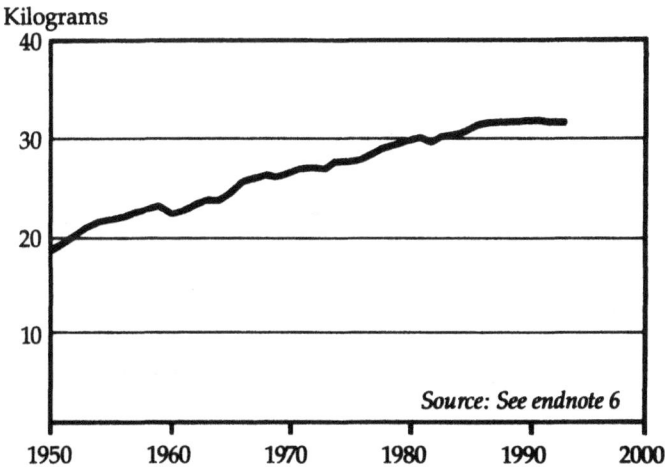

FIGURE 4-1. *World Meat Production Per Person, 1950–93*

step, rarely separated by much. But as that decade ended, pork surged ahead, largely on the strength of rapidly expanding grain supplies in China following the 1978 agricultural reforms. At the same time, the growth in beef production slowed. (See Figure 4–2.)[7]

With nearly all the world's rangeland now fully used (see Chapter 6), and with productivity falling in some situations because of overgrazing, the steady growth in beef output has been interrupted. The grazing capacity of rangelands has been pushed to the limit, so meaningful additions to the output of beef and mutton can only come from the feedlot. At this point, the relative conversion efficiencies of different meats begins to shape the pattern of meat production. For cattle in the feedlot, it takes roughly 7 kilograms of grain to add a kilogram of live weight. For pork, it takes roughly 4 kilograms. Poul-

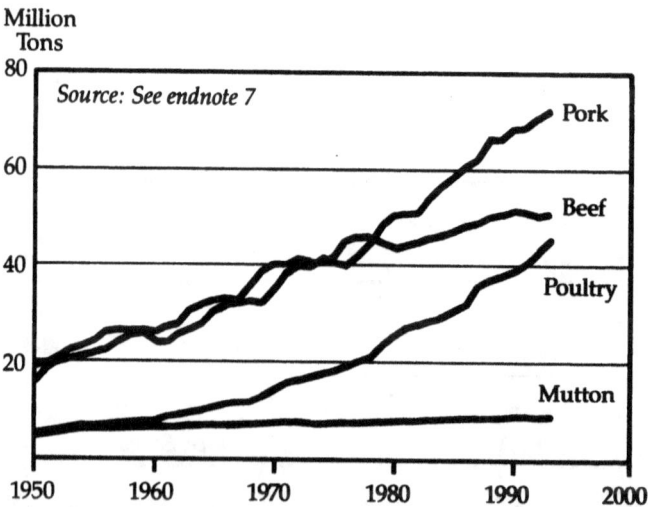

FIGURE 4-2. *World Meat Production by Type, 1950–93*

try and fish are even more efficient, requiring about 2 kilograms for each kilogram of live weight gain. Cheese and eggs are in between, requiring 3 and 2.6 kilograms of grain, respectively.[8]

With scarcely 2 kilograms of grain needed to produce a kilogram of weight gain in a well-managed broiler operation, world poultry production has moved to a new high each year since 1950, setting 43 consecutive annual records. Given this efficiency advantage, world poultry production will likely overtake that of beef before the end of this decade.[9]

As noted earlier, meat consumption varies widely among countries, ranging from 115 kilograms per person annually in the United States to only 1 kilogram in India. Australia trails closely behind the United States, with 104 kilograms. In France and Germany, consumption averages about 90 kilograms; in Brazil, Japan, and Mexico, it ranges between 40 and 47 kilograms. China's 1.2 billion people, further down the income ladder, eat an average of 26 kilograms each.[10]

In 1992, an estimated 635 million tons of grain were fed to livestock, poultry, and fish, accounting for 37 percent of the 1.72 billion tons of grain used worldwide. The share of the world's grain supply fed to animals increased steadily during the fifties and sixties, reaching an all-time high of 41 percent in 1972. Since then, it has changed little, fluctuating between 37 and 40 percent, with food and feed uses increasing at the same rate. (See Figure 4–3.)[11]

In per capita terms, world feedgrain use climbed from mid-century until 1986 when it peaked at 132 kilograms. From then until 1993 it dropped to 118 kilograms, a drop of 11 percent. (See Figure 4–4.) In part, this reflects a decline in consumption per person of beef,

Percent

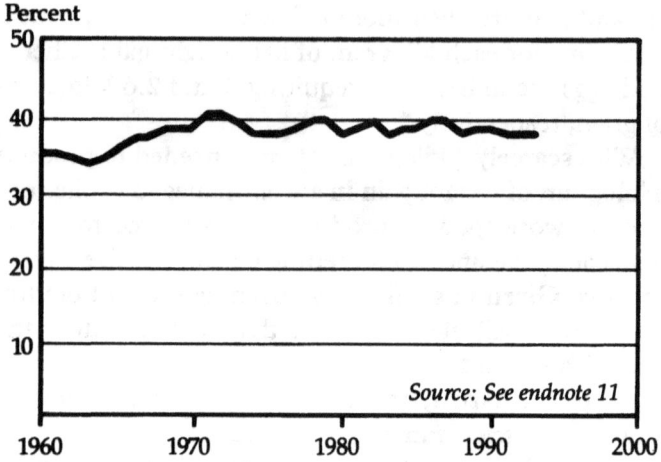

FIGURE 4-3. *Share of World Grain Used for Feed, 1960–93*

Kilograms

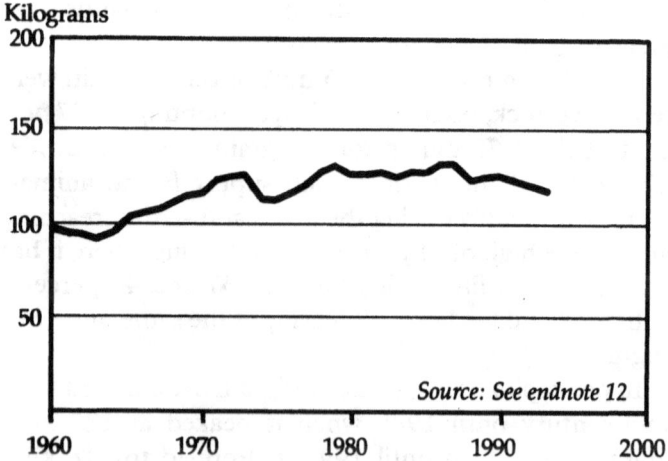

FIGURE 4-4. *World Per Capita Grain Fed to Livestock, 1960–93*

a particularly grain-intensive meat, and in part it reflects widespread efficiency gains in converting grain into livestock products.[12]

The share of grain used as feed varies widely by country. In Denmark, a heavy exporter of pork, some 82 percent of all grain is used for feed. In the European Union as a whole, it is 57 percent.[13]

Only when countries reach middle-income levels can they afford to feed more grain to livestock and poultry than to people. Brazil, for example, first crossed this threshold in 1979, when 51 percent of its grain was fed to animals. By 1990, the figure had edged up to 55 percent. In the rapidly growing economies of East Asia, the amount fed to animals is climbing steadily. In Taiwan, which exports pork, the figure has reached 62 percent, higher than in some European countries. In South Korea, another rapid-growth country, it climbed from just over 2 percent in 1960 to 39 percent in 1990.[14]

The share of grain fed to livestock in Mexico has gone from 5 percent in 1960 to 31 percent in 1990. During the same period, Japan climbed from 14 to 47 percent, a figure that would be even higher if large amounts of beef and pork were not imported. Growth in China's feed use has accelerated sharply since the economic reforms of 1978, when only 8 percent of grain was used for animal feed. By 1990, the figure had reached 20 percent, much of it for pork.[15]

In addition to limits on the growth in world consumption of livestock products imposed by the carrying capacity of rangelands and the slower growth in grain production, the availability of soybeans is also becoming a constraint. For livestock and poultry to use grain efficiently, a protein supplement is needed. The principal one for livestock feed is soybean meal, the residue remaining after the beans are crushed and the oil extracted. In the absence of protein supplements, livestock may need easily half again as much grain to produce a given amount of meat, milk, or eggs.

Originating in China, the soybean has found an ecological and economic niche in the western hemisphere. As recently as mid-century it was still something of a novelty crop, but rising affluence generated demand for livestock products, indirectly leading to rapid growth in the demand for soybean meal.

China's once dominant role in soybean production has been lost. The top three producers today are the United States, which produces half the crop, Brazil, and Argentina, leaving China in fourth place. In the United States, soybeans are one of the big three crops, along with corn and wheat. The value of the U.S. soybean harvest is now nearly twice that of the wheat harvest, putting it second behind corn.[16]

The worldwide constraint on expanding soybean production comes from the difficulty in raising yields. Whereas U.S. yields of corn have more than tripled since mid-century, those of soybeans—grown by the same farmers on the same land—have increased by scarcely half. For farmers, getting more soybeans depends mostly on planting more of them. This explains why recent growth in output is concentrated in land-abundant countries, like Brazil and Argentina, rather than in China.[17]

From 1950 until 1979, the world soybean harvest climbed from 18 million to 93 million tons, boosting per capita supplies from 7 kilograms to 21. But from 1979 to 1993 output climbed from 93 million to 111 million tons. So after averaging some 7 percent a year, growth dropped to less than 2 percent a year. Thus soybean production per person has ranged narrowly between 18 and 21 kilograms since 1979. If this figure cannot be raised, it will become much more difficult to increase the production of livestock products per person.[18]

If food supplies tighten in the years ahead, as now seems likely, the question of redistributing available food supplies becomes more urgent. Two questions arise: How much redistribution is possible? And how do we do it?

At present, the market portions out food, balancing supply and demand by adjusting price and distributing it according to purchasing power. With the dismantling of the centrally controlled food distribution systems in the former Soviet Union and China, the market now dominates more than ever. Except for the international food aid program, which accounts for roughly 1 percent of the world grain harvest, and national food assistance programs, such as India's fair price shops or the U.S. food stamp program, the market distributes food according to purchasing power. In this market-dominated food economy, a small handful of countries export grain; most of the remaining 160 import it.[19]

There are many reasons for the affluent to reduce their consumption of food, particularly meat. The desire to improve health offers an attractive reason for consuming less fat-rich livestock products, and hence the use of grain in affluent societies. The healthiest people in the world are neither those at the bottom of the grain ladder, whose diets are dominated by starches, nor those at the top who eat large amounts of livestock products. Far healthier are those in the middle. Italians, for example, live longer than Americans even though health expenditures per person are much greater in the United States.[20]

Concern for the environment provides another compelling reason to move down the food chain. The environmental advantages of consuming 400 kilograms of grain per year instead of 800 kilograms are obvious: less land, irrigation water, fertilizer, and pesticides are needed.

There are also humanitarian reasons for the affluent to consume less in order to make more food available for the poor. Other things being equal, lower consumption means lower food prices. Historically, food aid programs have been motivated by a mix of surplus reduction, political interest, and humanitarian concerns. In Chapter 14, we will return to the question of both the means and mechanisms for redistributing food.

The bottom line is that low-income people everywhere want to move up the food chain. The U.N. Food and Agriculture Organization projects that four fifths of the growth in feedgrain use by 2010 will occur in developing countries—170 million out of 215 million tons. The difference in diets between the world's rich and its poor is not a difference of values or desired diets, but one of means. As soon as the poor gain the purchasing power, they consume more animal protein. No developing-country government has ever said it would forgo the chance to raise consumption of meat, milk, and eggs. That all low-income societies want to consume more livestock products is a reality that policymakers cannot ignore.

II

The Three
Food Systems

5

Overharvesting the Oceans

In the early nineties, the state of the world's fisheries made newspaper headlines. They read "Too Few Fish in the Sea," "Overfishing Threatens To Wipe Out Species and Crush Industry," and "Ban on Industrial Fishing Called For." By 1992, many countries were acting to protect their fisheries. Canada suspended cod fishing entirely off the coast of Newfoundland, putting some 40,000 people out of work.[1]

In late 1993, Canada closed additional stretches of water to cod fishing, with the off-limits area creeping down toward the U.S. coast. The United States followed with restrictions designed to save its cod, haddock, and flounder fisheries off New England. "Fishermen Beached As Harvest Dries Up," reported the *Washington Post* in March 1994, as strict quotas kept boats in dock.[2]

On the West coast, conditions are no better. In April 1994, the Pacific Fishery Management Council banned salmon fishing off Washington state for the first time in an effort to have enough salmon survive to continue the species. In Oregon and California, stringent salmon quotas were imposed. Actions by these two leading fishing countries, combined with innumerable similar measures taken by governments elsewhere, amount to an acknowledgment that many fisheries have been exploited to their limits and that further harvesting could destroy a valuable food source.[3]

These steps are reversing the trend of recent decades. A global seafood harvest of some 22 million tons in 1950 ballooned to 100 million tons in 1989, providing food and economic growth around the world. From less than 9 kilograms of fish per person at mid-century, the catch rose to more than 19 kilograms by 1989. For the average person, seafood consumption more than doubled.[4]

But fish stocks declined in a number of key areas during the eighties. The 1990 global catch weighed in at 3 million tons below the previous year, and population growth quickly outpaced the production of fisheries. The 1991 and 1992 catches remained at 97 million tons, and the 1993 catch was estimated at 98 million tons, still well below the 1989 peak. (See Figure 5–1.) Per capita fish supplies are down to 17.6 kilograms, a drop of 8 percent from the historical high.[5]

As noted in Chapter 1, according to the marine scientists at the U.N. Food and Agriculture Organization (FAO), all 17 of the world's major fishing regions are currently harvested at or beyond their capacity. Nine are in a state of decline. Without careful management to maintain existing stocks, the catches will decline further.[6]

Million
Tons

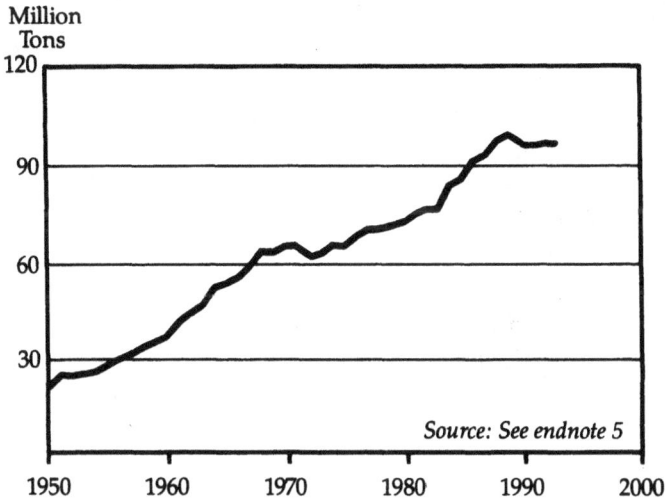

FIGURE 5-1. *World Fish Catch, 1950–93*

During the seventies and eighties, many governments subsidized fishing fleets, providing large loans and favorable terms for those willing to buy new boats with efficient new technologies. By 1990, however, those loans had become unsupportable, as catches dwindled and quotas kept fishers on shore during what used to be peak fishing months.[7]

Fisheries subsidies were based on an unfounded belief that past trends in oceanic harvests could be projected into the future—that past growth meant future growth. The long-standing advice of FAO marine biologists, who had said that the marine harvest would someday reach a limit, was mostly ignored.

That attitude has proved costly. Excessive demand directly threatens the productivity of oceanic fisheries. For countries like Canada, Iceland, and Japan, overfishing has led to a net loss of seafood harvested rather than a gain. Most traditional marine fish stocks are fully exploited, meaning that additional harvesting will reduce their numbers. Atlantic stocks of the heavily fished bluefin tuna have been cut by a staggering 94 percent. It will take years for such species to recover, even if fishing stops altogether.[8]

Dwindling fish stocks are affecting many national economies. In Canada, for example—where the fishing industry traditionally landed roughly 1.5 million tons a year, worth $3.1 billion—depletion of the cod and haddock fisheries off the coast of Nova Scotia has led to shrinking catches and heavy layoffs in the fishing and fish processing industries. To cushion the massive job loss in the industry, which is the mainstay of Newfoundland's economy, Ottawa authorized a $400-million aid package for unemployment compensation and retraining.[9]

As overfishing of the North Atlantic by U.S., Canadian, and European fleets decimated stocks during the seventies, the ships turned to the South Atlantic, particularly the fisheries off the African coast. Prior to controlling fishing in the 200-mile Exclusive Economic Zones granted by the 1979 Law of the Sea Treaty, some African countries saw their fish stocks decimated. Namibia, for instance, watched the catch in its zone fall from nearly 2 million tons in 1980 to less than 100,000 tons a decade later. After banning European ships from its waters in 1990, stocks started to recover.[10]

Fisheries are a particularly important source of food and animal protein for countries with long coastlines and for island nations. Land-scarce countries also rely heavily on seafood for protein since they have little capacity to raise livestock or poultry. (See Table 5-1.)

TABLE 5-1. *Annual Seafood Consumption Per Person in Selected Countries, Mid-Eighties*

Country	Seafood	Country	Seafood
	(kilograms of live weight)		(kilograms of live weight)
Japan	69	Mexico	10
South Korea	51	Argentina	7
Philippines	34	Turkey	7
Spain	33	Bangladesh	7
Soviet Union	28	China	6
France	26	Brazil	6
Canada	22	Nigeria	6
Thailand	22	Egypt	6
United States	19	Kenya	5
United Kingdom	19	Algeria	4
Poland	19	India	3
Italy	18	Iran	3
Australia	17	Pakistan	2
Indonesia	14	Sudan	1
Vietnam	12	Ethiopia	0.1

SOURCE: See endnote 11.

Japan's fish and rice diet evolved as population pressures intensified, leaving little land to produce feed for livestock and poultry.[11]

Inland fisheries are also suffering from environmental mismanagement—water diversion, acidification, and pollution. The Aral Sea, located between Kazakhstan and Uzbekistan, as recently as 1960 yielded 40,000 tons of fish per year. Shrinking steadily over the last three decades as the river water feeding it was diverted for irrigation, the sea has become increasingly salty, eventually destroying the fish stock. Biologically, it is now effectively dead. A similar situation exists in Pakistan, where Deg Nullah, a small but once highly productive freshwater lake that yielded 400 tons of fish annually, is now barren—destroyed by pollution. Acidification is also taking a toll. Canada alone now counts 14,000 dead lakes.[12]

In the United States, pollution has severely affected the Chesapeake Bay, one of the world's richest estuaries. Its fabulously productive oyster beds, which yielded 8 million bushels a year a century ago, now produce around 300,000 bushels. Elsewhere, fish have survived, such as in the U.S. Great Lakes and New York's Hudson River, but are unsafe for human consumption because of pollution with polychlorinated biphenyls (PCBs) and other toxic chemicals. Half the shellfish-growing areas off Nova Scotia in eastern Canada have been closed because of contamination.[13]

With already available data on fisheries, it is now possible to project future fish harvests per person. Given that all the major regional seas are at or beyond their capacity, it is reasonable to take a figure near today's harvest as a point of departure. Using the round number of 100 million tons, which is quite close to today's catch, and the population projections discussed earlier, it is clear that the fish supply per person will decrease in coming years. By 2030 it will have fallen to about 11 kilograms per person, not much more than around mid-century. (See Figure 5–2.) Hence, the next four decades could essentially see a reversal of the trend of the last four. The years when fish harvests outpaced human population growth are being replaced by years when the opposite is true.[14]

Two wildcards exist in this calculation. The first concerns reduced waste and improved management, which will somewhat increase the amount of food available. As discussed later in this chapter, it is possible to raise the

Kilograms

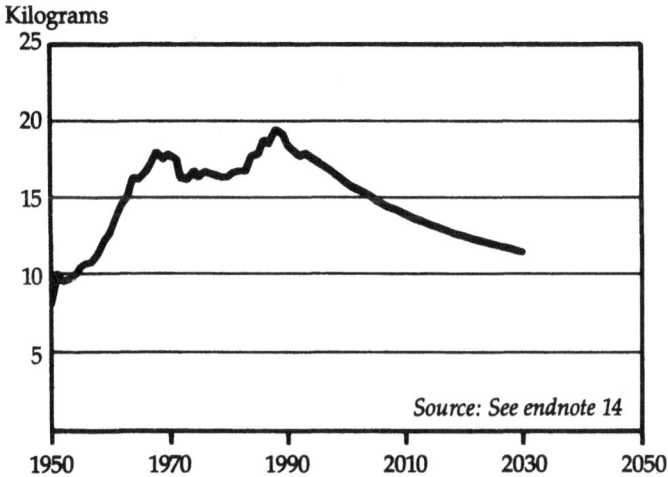

FIGURE 5-2. *World Fish Catch Per Person, 1950–93, With Projections to 2030*

catch by taking care not to waste "bycatch" or throw away the less desirable parts of fish. Learning how to harvest waters at their maximum sustainable levels without surpassing those levels can also boost the catch modestly.

The second wildcard is aquaculture, or fish farming. By feeding grain to fish in ponds or cages, the global harvest can be expanded without some of the constraints on wild harvests from oceans, rivers, and lakes. Yet aquaculture production is constrained by competition for grain, scarce water, and, for some species, scarce waterfront land. For purposes of this projection, we assume aquaculture production to remain around the 12.7 million tons of today (16 million tons if aquatic plants are included). In fact, fish farming will almost certainly expand further in the late nineties—but thereafter growing scarcities of grain needed for feed and of land and water will hold it back, so the projection offered here is a reasonable ballpark estimate.[15]

Moreover, several other marine trends are acting to counter any gains realized by improved management or aquaculture. The spawning grounds and nurseries of many aquatic creatures are being lost, for example. Some 90 percent (by mass) of marine animals rely on coastal areas such as wetlands, mangrove swamps, or rivers for spawning grounds. But well over half the original area of mangroves in tropical countries has been lost, and in industrial countries, the rate for wetlands loss is just as high. In Italy, whose coastal wetlands are the nurseries for the Mediterranean fisheries, it is a staggering 95 percent.[16]

A third of the world's urban population lives within 60 kilometers of a coastline, a big contributor to the pollution that reaches the seas. Sewage, fertilizers, and runoff from agriculture have overfed algae, causing it to "bloom" in a rapid growth that uses up the oxygen that fish need to breathe. Estimates of global annual discharge into rivers range from 7 million to 35 million tons of nitrogen and from 600,000 to 3.75 million tons of dissolved phosphorus. Thus the carrying capacity of coastal areas has been far exceeded, both by people who live there and by those living in other regions who buy coastal harvests and whose wastes and pollutants come from afar to degrade marine habitats.[17]

Stratospheric ozone depletion that lets through more ultraviolet radiation also affects life in the sea. The photosynthesis and growth of phytoplankton, which are the lowest link of the food chain, have decreased by as much as 20 percent near the surface of Antarctic waters—the area where most marine growth and reproduction takes place. Global warming also may touch sea life deeply because it could alter ocean currents, which circulate heat and vital nutrients. (See Chapter 11.)[18]

Thus, even with improved management and aquaculture, per capita fish supplies can be expected to fall almost to their 1950 levels by 2030. After more than doubling the amount of fish available per person between 1950 and 1989, fisheries can no longer provide dietary diversity and nutritional gain.

The use of fishing technology has had a peculiar history. For many years, oceanic harvests expanded as new tools were invented, from sonar for tracking fish to purse seine nets for pulling in massive catches. The rising world commercial catch from the fifties into the eighties is partly a story of larger boats, on-board processing capabilities, and vast drift nets collectively large enough to circle the earth many times over. But the stagnating world commercial catch of the early nineties is also a story of those same factory trawlers and mammoth traps.

After a point, expanded fishing capacity led to overfishing that reduced the following year's harvest even as it increased the day's catch. Technologies were overused, and instead of continuing to yield more food, they caused a collapse of some fish stocks, such as Canada's cod fishery. Catches declined even when fishers had expected them to increase. Commercial fishing is now largely an economics of today versus tomorrow. Governments are seeking to protect tomorrow's catches by forcing fishers to keep their ships idle; fishing communities are torn between the need for income and food today and in the future. "With more powerful boats and fish finders, we basically have the capacity to wipe fish out, and we are," warns Douglas Foy of the Conservation Law Foundation in New England.[19]

This is a real dilemma for those who think that food supplies will always increase if human ingenuity is unleashed and if harvests can earn high bids in the marketplace. The solutions relied on by colleagues in other industries, such as the pursuit of more effective ways of producing, will not come to their aid. Instead, fishery management has become a task of matching harvesting capacity with natural supplies. Quotas have become the rule of the day, and they are enforced by police ships, helicopters, and surveillance planes.

Without these seemingly drastic measures, there would be a danger not only of short-term impoverishment of fishing communities but also of lasting losses to fishing industries. Severe overfishing can even change the composition of marine life, as some species gain advantages over others. When that happens, a species can compete more effectively for food supplies, and that makes it difficult for a degraded species to recover. It is not possible to predict the consequences of a change in species, but fishers who have relied on particular fish for generations have cause to fear such changes.

Although technology cannot abolish limits to marine food supplies, it can help reduce wastes in the harvest. One such potential stems from the enormous quantities of fish waste thrown overboard from factory trawlers or discarded at processing plants. Better techniques of cleaning fish could salvage up to 15 percent of the total consumed today. And better knowledge of which schools of fish are large enough to bear harvesting and which schools are better left alone would optimize the tonnage of marine life taken each year. Furthermore, aquacultural technology can be used to optimize the use of the world's feedgrains, because fish farmers can convert grain to animal protein more efficiently than beef and pork producers can.[20]

Fish are cold-blooded, so they do not burn calories to keep themselves warm, and they need minimal muscle to move around in the water searching for food. That makes them particularly efficient at converting grain into animal protein. Catfish, for example, one of the most efficient species, require 2 kilograms or less of feed to yield a kilogram of weight; by contrast, as noted in Chapter 4, cattle in the feedlot require 7 kilograms of grain per kilogram of gain in the feedlot, pigs need roughly 4 kilograms, and broilers, just over 2.[21]

As the catches from the open oceans and the inland lakes and rivers have slowed, the attractiveness of fish farming has increased. Worldwide, the controlled raising of fish in ocean pens and inland ponds or tanks has grown from 6.7 million tons in 1984 to 12.7 million tons in 1991 (excluding aquatic plants). (See Figure 5–3.) That is one eighth of the total catch.[22]

But aquaculture has its own problems. The easy spread of disease among fish kept in tight quarters, the spread of that disease to wild stocks by fish that escape the pens, inbreeding and genetic weakening of natural stocks, pollution by fish wastes, and market stability are all matters of concern. Irish stocks of wild sea trout collapsed in 1989, for example, falling to less than 10 percent of their ordinary levels because of infestations of sea lice, a parasite almost unheard of until salmon farming started in the area in the mid-eighties. From Maine to Norway, production of salmon and other farmed fish has flourished and then occasionally been devastated, sometimes by disease, sometimes by competition from other producers.[23]

As historical growth in the amount of food taken from

**Million
Tons**

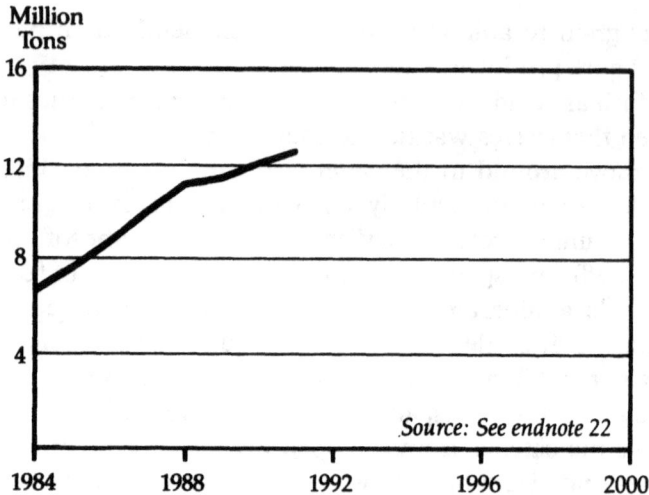

FIGURE 5-3. *World Aquacultural Production, 1984–91*

the seas diminished while the number of people and their demand for seafood continued to rise, it was not surprising that seafood prices rose. Some of the best data on seafood prices are from the United States, where what was once a cheap source of high-quality protein is now one of the most expensive. U.S. seafood prices were 40 percent higher in the early nineties than in 1950, after adjusting for inflation, with nearly all the rise coming since 1970. (Prices of beef, by comparison, were down by more than one fourth over that period and those of poultry fell by two thirds.) (See Figure 5–4.)[24]

As noted earlier, what is ironic about the rising prices for seafood is that dramatic improvements in fishing technology during those years were expected to lead to the opposite result. With chicken, for example, the decline in the U.S. price came despite almost a doubling in demand since the late sixties, because new technologies

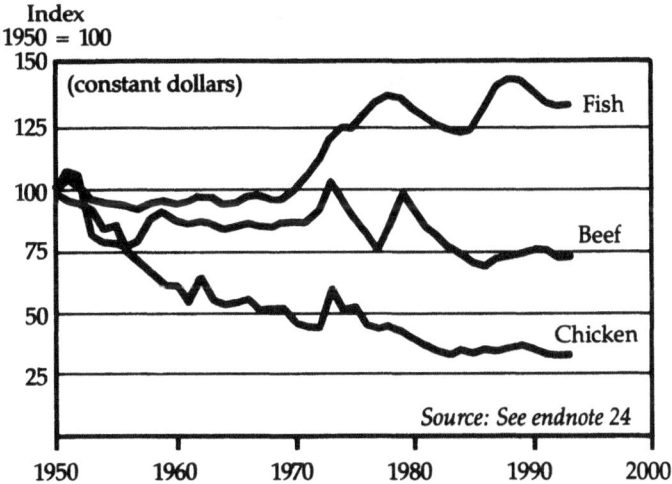

FIGURE 5-4. *U.S. Price of Fish, Beef, and Chicken, 1950–93*

greatly expanded the output of broilers. But with fish, a point was reached in many seas where fish were harvested faster than they could reproduce, and stocks declined.[25]

In some developing countries, the effect of higher seafood prices has been for the catch to leave local markets for those of industrial countries. The tonnage of seafood exports from developing nations has grown by three fourths in volume since 1981. Until 1988, the European Community was self-sufficient in fish and shellfish (though some of that was caught off the coasts of developing countries), but rising consumption has now forced European nations to import. In Japan, imports of seafood rose from $4 billion in 1985 to $10 billion in 1990. These trends will take fish away from local consumption in the Third World.[26]

Thus what happens to seafood prices in countries like

the United States affects consumption of seafood in many other regions as well. Growing income from fish exports may help the trade balances of indebted countries, but if it increases protein malnutrition, it will have done little for the poorest groups in those societies.

World consumption of fish exceeds that of beef and chicken combined. In some countries, fish provides most of the animal protein consumed. Yet among the finite ecosystems that must supply growing human populations with food, fisheries have suffered the most sudden loss of momentum. The moribund state of the world's fisheries is thus one of the first signals of a tightening world food supply.[27]

6

Overgrazing Rangelands

Eleven percent of the world's land area is used to produce crops, but an area twice this size is in rangeland—land that is either too dry or too steeply sloping to be cultivated. This one fifth of the world's land area supports most of the world's 3.2 billion cattle, sheep, and goats—at least one for every two people in the world. (See Table 6–1.) These animals are ruminants; they have digestive systems of four stomachs that enable them to thrive on roughage, converting it into the meat and milk that is consumed by billions of people, many of them in Third World pastoral economies.[1]

Such economies, mainly in North Africa, the Sahelian zone, East Africa, and much of Southern Africa, depend on their livestock economies for sustenance and employment. The same is true for large populations in the Mid-

TABLE 6-1. *World Domestic Ruminant Resources, by Region, 1990*

Region	Cattle	Sheep and Goats	Water Buffalo	Total
		(million)		
North America	110	14	—	124
Latin America	323	155	1	479
Europe	124	165	—	289
Soviet Union	118	145	—	263
Oceania	32	230	—	262
Africa	190	392	3	585
Asia	396	702	134	1,232
World	1,293	1,803	138	3,234

SOURCE: See endnote 1.

dle East and the Central Asian Republics. India, which has the world's largest concentration of ruminants (270 million head of cattle and water buffalo and 117 million goats), is particularly dependent on cattle and water buffalo not only for milk but also for draft power and food.[2]

Australia, whose land mass is dominated by range-land, has the world's largest sheep flock—147 million, or 8 sheep for each Australian. Grass-based livestock economies also predominate in Brazil, Argentina, Uruguay, and Mexico. And in the Great Plains of North America, lands that are not suited to growing wheat are devoted to grazing cattle.[3]

Most of the world's beef and mutton is produced on rangeland; only a small fraction actually comes from weight added in feedlots. The share of the world's cattle, sheep, and goats in feedlots at any time is relatively small compared with the vast numbers feeding on grass, even in the United States.

Beef and mutton tend to dominate meat consumption where grazing land is abundant relative to population size. Among the countries leading beef consumption per person are Uruguay (72 kilograms of beef measured in carcass weight consumed per year), Argentina (70 kilograms), the United States (44 kilograms), Australia (38 kilograms), Canada (35 kilograms), New Zealand (34 kilograms), and Brazil (25 kilograms). In some countries with extensive grazing land, mutton looms large in the diet—as in New Zealand (26 kilograms), Australia (20 kilograms), Kyrgyzstan (13 kilograms), and Kazakhstan (10 kilograms).[4]

In many countries, the herds of cattle and flocks of sheep and goats that live on the range are a major source of protein, in the form of both meat and milk. Although attention typically focuses on the amount of protein coming from rangelands, in many countries meat and milk account for a large share of food energy intake.

These same ruminants that are so uniquely efficient at converting roughage into usable foodstuffs for people are also a major source of raw materials. The world's leather goods and wool industries, a source of livelihood for millions, depend heavily on rangelands for their raw materials.

World beef and mutton production, totalling an estimated 24 million tons in 1950, reached 62 million tons in 1990 and then dropped to 60 million tons in 1993. The per capita trend over the last four decades breaks into two distinct periods. It rose from 1950 until 1972, climbing from 9.3 kilograms to 12.7 kilograms, a gain of 37 percent. From 1972 until 1993, however, the growth in beef and mutton production has not kept pace with population growth, so per capita supplies dropped to 11 kilograms. (See Figure 6–1.)[5]

The reason for this loss of momentum is that growing herds of cattle and flocks of sheep and goats are now exceeding the carrying capacity of rangelands in many countries. As a result, the growth in numbers in many cases has come to an end, and in some places has actually declined as grazing lands have deteriorated. This excessive pressure, not unlike that on oceanic fisheries, afflicts industrial and developing countries alike. A 1990 survey of U.S. grazing lands managed by the Bureau of Land Management, for example, showed only 33 percent to be in good or excellent condition, with most of the remainder in fair to poor condition.[6]

The comparatively slow growth in output of beef since the mid-seventies reflects the constraints imposed

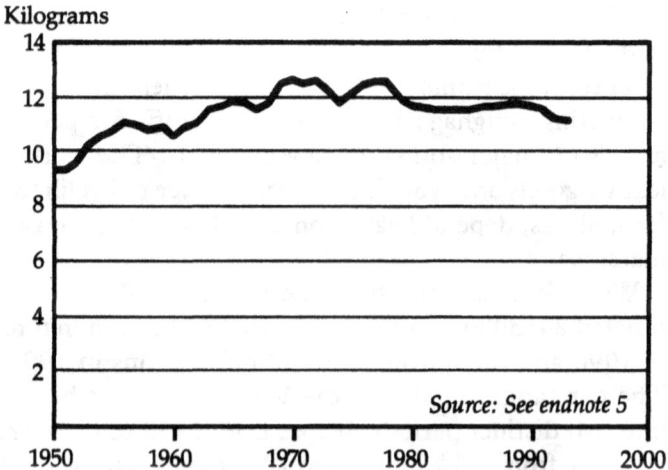

Kilograms

Source: See endnote 5

FIGURE 6-1. *World Beef and Mutton Production Per Person, 1950–93*

by the earth's grazing capacity limits. Since 1950, beef production has expanded just 2.7 times, going from 19 million to 52 million tons. Growth in mutton production, including both sheep and goats, has been even slower, scarcely doubling. These animals are concentrated in semiarid regions such as North Africa, the Middle East, the Central Asian Republics, the Indian subcontinent, and Australia—all regions that suffer from extensive overgrazing.[7]

Although the data for grassland degradation are sparse, the trends are no less real. This problem is highly visible throughout Africa, where livestock numbers have expanded nearly as fast as the human population. In 1950, 238 million Africans relied on 273 million livestock. By 1993, the human population had increased to 665 million while that of livestock reached 564 million.[8]

In a continent where grain is scarce, 190 million cattle, 206 million sheep, and 168 million goats are supported almost entirely by grazing and browsing. Everywhere outside the tsetse-fly belt, livestock are vital to the economy. But in many countries their numbers exceed grassland carrying capacity by half or more. A study charting the mounting pressures on grasslands in nine southern African countries found that the capacity to sustain livestock is diminishing. As grasslands deteriorate, soil erosion accelerates, further reducing the carrying capacity and setting in motion a self-reinforcing cycle of ecological degradation and deepening human poverty.[9]

Fodder needs of livestock in nearly all developing countries now exceed the sustainable yield of rangelands and other forage resources. In India, the demand for fodder by the end of the decade is expected to reach 700 million tons annually, while the supply will total just 540 million tons. The National Land Use and Wastelands Development Council there reports that in states with the most serious land degradation, such as Rajasthan and Karnataka, fodder supplies satisfy only 50–80 percent of needs, leaving large numbers of emaciated, unproductive cattle. When drought occurs, hundreds of thousands of these animals die. In drought years, local governments in India have established fodder relief camps for cattle threatened with starvation, not unlike the food relief camps set up for people threatened with famine.[10]

Land degradation from overgrazing is taking a heavy economic toll in the form of lost livestock productivity. In the early stages of overgrazing, the costs show up as lower land productivity. But if the process continues unarrested, it eventually creates wasteland as the destruction of vegetation eventually leads to the loss of soil through wind and water erosion and extensive land degradation. Using data for 1990, a U.N. assessment of the earth's dryland regions showed that lost livestock production as a result of rangeland degradation totalled $23.2 billion in that year. (See Table 6–2.)[11]

In Africa, where this problem is most visible, the annual loss of rangeland productivity is estimated at $7 billion, more than the gross national product of Ethiopia and Uganda combined. In Asia, livestock losses from rangeland degradation total $8.3 billion. Together, Africa and Asia account for just over $15 billion out of the $23.2 billion total.[12]

The effects of overgrazing on rangeland productivity are becoming visible at the global level. Between 1990 and 1993, world production of beef fell nearly 3 percent, while mutton was unchanged. In per capita terms, beef production fell nearly 8 percent during this three-year

TABLE 6-2. *Annual Losses in Livestock Production from Land Degradation in Dryland Regions*

Continent	Rangeland
	(billion dollars)
Africa	7.0
Asia	8.3
Australia	2.5
Europe	0.6
North America	2.9
South America	2.1
Total[1]	23.2

[1]Columns may not add up to totals due to rounding.

SOURCE: See endnote 11.

period while mutton dropped 5 percent.[13]

The prospect for substantial future gains in beef and mutton production are not good. With most rangeland now being grazed at capacity or beyond it, substantial further gains in beef and mutton production can come only from the feedlot. But this source is not promising either, because in the competition for scarce grain, the more efficient converters—including pork and particularly poultry—have a decided advantage. In a world with little additional grain for livestock feeding, there may not be much growth at all in beef and mutton production in the decades ahead.

7

Limits of
the Plow

From the beginning of agriculture in the Middle East until the mid-twentieth century, cropland area expanded as agriculture spread from valley to valley and then from continent to continent. Throughout this period, growth in food output came largely from expanding the cultivated area.

This era ended in the mid-twentieth century as the frontiers of agricultural settlement disappeared. From then until 1981, there were some modest gains in harvested area, but four fifths of the growth in output came from raising land productivity. The method of expanding food output had shifted dramatically almost overnight. In 1981, grainland area peaked at 735 million hectares. Then it began to shrink, dropping to 695 million hectares in 1993.[1]

Thus the history of agricultural yields divides neatly into three periods: a time of expanding area until around mid-century, a time of mostly expanding yields with some modest growth in area until 1981, and a time when all additional output has come from raising land productivity. (See Figure 7–1.)[2]

There are still occasional increases in cropland area here and there. Brazil, for example, more than doubled its area in grain between 1960 and 1980. Since then, however, its grainland has not expanded significantly. A few countries are expanding grain-harvested area by multiple cropping—combining, for example, winter wheat with a summer rice crop. On balance, however, these gains are offset by losses as cropland is converted to nonfarm uses or abandoned because of severe degradation.[3]

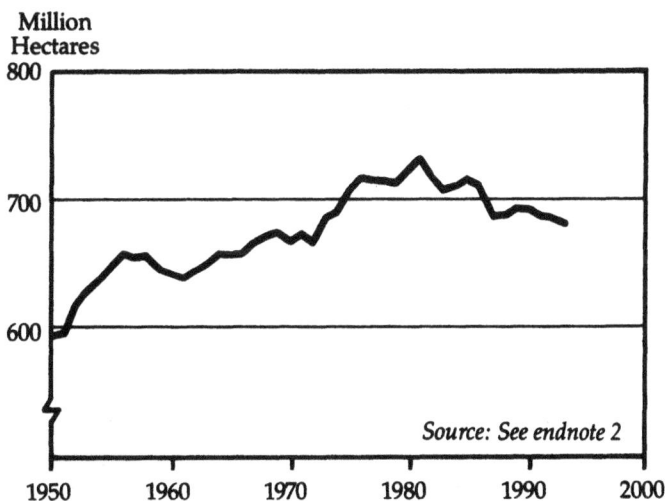

FIGURE 7-1. *World Grain Harvested Area, 1950–93*

Worldwide, gains in cropland area from year to year are the result of various cropland expansion initiatives, including the conversion of forest, new irrigation projects that permit the farming of land otherwise too dry to farm, and drainage of wetlands. Forest conversion is concentrated in such places as the outer islands of Indonesia (part of a long-term resettlement program of people from densely populated Java) and the Amazon regions of Brazil and other Latin American countries. Some of these gains are illusory, since this land will often sustain cultivation for only a few years before losing its natural fertility.

Some of the most important gains have come from the adoption of high-yielding, early maturing wheats and rices that spurred the spread of multiple cropping. Traditional geography texts contained agricultural maps with a line drawn across both India and China, separating the wheat- and rice-growing regions. Modern maps do not make that distinction: wheat has extended into rice-growing areas and vice versa, with rice being grown in the summer and wheat in the winter. Earlier maturing varieties of both grains, combined with the spread of irrigation that facilitated dry-season farming, helped increase double-cropping. For example, of the 130 million hectares of rice land in Asia, 12 million hectares now also produce a winter wheat crop.[4]

Between 1972 and 1981, farmers responded to sustained high prices by expanding the world grain area from 664 million to 735 million hectares, a gain of nearly 11 percent. Much of this increase came in the former Soviet Union and the United States on land that, unfortunately, was highly erodible and not capable of sustaining cultivation. After peaking at 123 million hectares in 1977, the Soviet Union's grain harvested area has declined almost every year, dropping to 99 million hectares in 1993 as fast-eroding land was either planted to soil-stabilizing forage crops, fallowed, or abandoned. In the United States, some 14 million hectares of the most erodible cropland were converted to grass or trees between 1985 and 1992 under the Conservation Reserve Program. In an emergency, some of this land could be farmed in rotation with forage crops or by using other appropriate conservation tillage practices.[5]

All grainland held out under commodity supply management programs in the United States was released for production in 1994. European countries may be holding out up to 3 million hectares. But even bringing all this land back would expand the world grain area by only 1.6 percent, not half enough to get it back to the historical high reached in 1981. The continuing abandonment of severely eroded land and the conversion of cropland to nonfarm uses means that net gains in the world's cropland area will not come easily.[6]

Some of the world's cropland is plagued by political problems rather than agronomic ones. These areas might be brought into production sometime in the future. Wars, ethnic conflicts, and discrimination that prevent farmers from working the land are no less real than problems of soil fertility or lack of water. Southern Sudan is one example of a food-deficit region that could feed itself if given the opportunity. But it has suffered from almost unbroken war in recent years.

The shifting of land to nonfarm uses is particularly pronounced in China, which is losing nearly 1 million hectares or 1 percent of its cropland a year. One result of the prosperity since economic reforms were launched in 1978 is that literally millions of villagers are either expanding their houses or building new ones. And an average annual industrial growth rate of more than 12 percent since 1980 means the construction of thousands of new factories. Sales of cars and trucks, totalling 1.2 million in 1992 and projected at close to 3 million by decade's end, will chew up cropland for roads and parking lots. Since most of China's nearly 1.2 billion people are concentrated in its rich farming regions, new homes and factories are of necessity often built on cropland. This loss, combined with a shift to more profitable crops, has reduced the grain harvested area in China by roughly one tenth from the recent peak in 1976.[7]

Urban sprawl is also claiming cropland. In Thailand, the expansion of Bangkok, driven by both prosperity and population growth, has claimed an average of 3,200 hectares each year during the past decade. Similarly, in Egypt, new building invariably comes at the expense of cropland, since the nation's 58 million people live on the thin ribbon of irrigated cropland along the Nile River.[8]

The requirements of some 90 million additional people each year for housing, schools, and transportation reduces the area available for crops worldwide. Land claimed by expanding transportation systems is particularly extensive. For example, the growth in the world automobile fleet means cropland is paved over for streets, highways, and parking lots. Some 200 square feet is needed merely to park an automobile. If a car is to be widely used, parking spaces must be available in many different places: near residences, workplaces, shops, and recreation areas. Assuming a minimum of two parking spaces per car, the land required to park 100 cars could easily produce one ton of grain per year, enough to feed five people. Observing the difficulty in reversing this process, a U.S. government official once remarked, "Asphalt is the land's last crop."[9]

Cropland is also being lost indirectly through the growing diversion of irrigation water to cities in desert areas. In Arizona, for example, Tucson and Phoenix have purchased the irrigation rights to large areas of cropland, letting it go back to desert. Even this may be dwarfed by the diversion of irrigation water to cities in northern China.[10]

The loss of cropland can be seen clearly in East Asia, particularly in the countries like Japan, South Korea, and Taiwan that were densely populated before industrialization began. In Japan, the loss was already under way by 1960, when the nation harvested 5 million hectares of grain. That figure now stands just above 2.5 million hectares. South Korea's grain area grew during the early sixties to more than 2.3 million hectares, and then fell steadily, dropping to just 1.3 million hectares in 1993. Taiwan experienced a similar drop, from 850,000 hectares in 1975 to only 500,000 today. (See Figure 7-2.)[11]

As factories, roads, and houses eat up land, and as relatively high wages in manufacturing industries pull labor away from farms, these trends in falling grainland area can be expected to continue. Even countries like Thailand that have had less success than South Korea and Taiwan at industrialization are seeing their grainland areas slip. Thailand's grew steadily until 1985, but it has since shrunk by more than 10 percent. India, which is projected to pass China to become the world's most populated nation near the middle of the next century, has watched its grainland area shrink from a peak of 107 million hectares in 1982 to 102 million in 1993.[12]

Future cropland losses are likely to be concentrated in Asia, with gains in Latin America. Losses will likely be heavy in Asia simply because that is where most of the

Million
Hectares

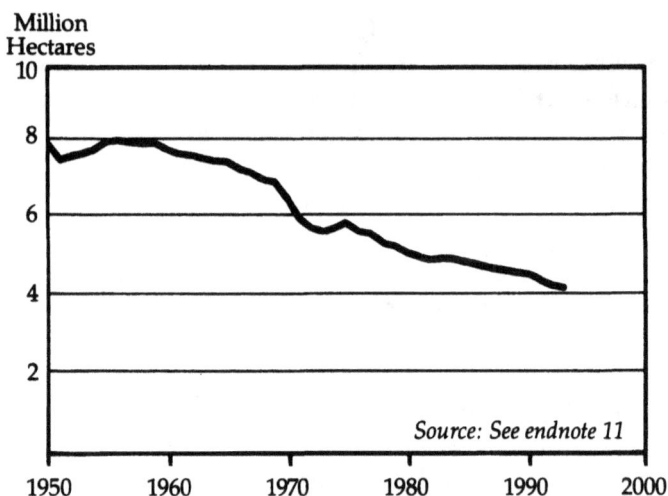

Source: See endnote 11

FIGURE 7-2. *Combined Grain Area, Japan, South Korea, and Taiwan, 1950–93*

population growth and industrialization are expected to occur. Gains will come mostly in Latin America because that is the region where there are extensive areas of land—albeit marginal—to be brought under production.

Unfortunately, the cropland lost in Asia will be highly productive for the most part, whereas that gained in Latin America will be marginal. The largest single area of cropland loss will likely be in Southern China, where much of the land is now being used to double-crop rice. In effect, land producing eight tons of milled rice per hectare annually will be replaced with marginal land in Brazil that will produce at most three tons of corn per hectare.[13]

Land will also be lost from soil erosion, much of it in

Africa. Waterlogging and salinity will take a toll in the Asian republics around the Aral Sea and in the Middle East, India, China, and the southwestern United States.

With 3.6 billion people slated to be added to world population between 1990 and 2030, the cropland area per person will continue to shrink steadily. From 1950 to 1990, it fell from 0.23 hectares per person to 0.13 hectares. (See Figure 7–3.) If the total grainland area does not change, by 2030 it will drop to 0.08 hectares per person.[14]

From 1950 to 1990 the shrinkage in grainland per person was not a threat, since farmers could substitute fertilizer for land. With the response to the use of fertilizer dropping so precipitously in recent years, even in many developing countries, this option is fast disappearing for many. In a nutshell, the challenge facing govern-

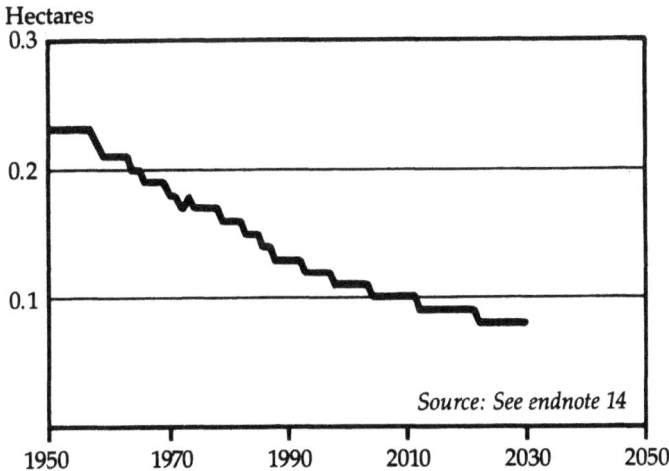

FIGURE 7-3. *World Grainland Per Person, 1950–93, With Projections to 2030*

ments is to find ways to offset the continued shrinkage in cropland area per person with new methods of raising land productivity.

Projecting future grainland availability per person in the more populous countries during the next four decades is revealing. (See Table 7–1.) In 1990, the smallest areas of grainland per person were in Egypt, with 0.04 hectares per person, and in Indonesia and Ethiopia, each with 0.07 hectares. Even though all of Egypt's grainland is irrigated, it imports half its grain supply. Indonesia, with a large share of irrigated land, is nearly self-sufficient. Ethiopia, with the same land area

TABLE 7-1. *Grain Harvested Area Per Person, by Country, 1950 and 1990, With Projections to 2030*

Country	1950	1990	2030[1]
		(hectares)	
China	0.17	0.08	0.06
United States	0.53	0.26	0.22
India	0.22	0.12	0.07
Former Soviet Union	0.57	0.35	0.27
Bangladesh	0.20	0.10	0.05
Pakistan	0.18	0.10	0.04
Indonesia	0.07	0.07	0.04
Iran	0.21	0.17	0.06
Egypt	0.08	0.04	0.02
Ethiopia & Eritrea	0.24	0.07	0.02
Nigeria	0.23	0.09	0.03
Brazil	0.13	0.14	0.07
Mexico	0.20	0.11	0.06

[1]Assumes no change in total grain harvested area from 1990 to 2030; reductions in area per person due entirely to population growth.

SOURCE: See endnote 15.

per person, almost all of it rainfed, is struggling to keep its people alive, even with an annual food aid allotment of 1 million tons of grain.[15]

In 2030, if the countries are able to maintain the same total grainland area, only one developing country listed in Table 7–1 will have as much as 0.07 hectares per person. All the others will have less, with Egypt and Ethiopia dropping down to 0.02 hectares. For Egypt, this will undoubtedly translate into even greater dependence on imports. For Ethiopia, a grainland area per person of 0.02 hectares—less than a third of that today—can only be described as catastrophic. The same can be said for Nigeria, with only 0.03 hectares per person.

It is this reduction in cropland per person that argues strongly for individual country assessments of population carrying capacity. Faced with such a threatening shrinkage of grainland, people living in these countries may opt to shift much more quickly to smaller families.

III

Losing
Momentum

8

Spreading Water
Scarcity

Perhaps not entirely by coincidence, early civilizations and irrigation appear to have evolved together, making the diversion of river water onto land one of civilization's earliest achievements. Thus it comes at no surprise that the decline of early civilizations in the Middle East coincided with the deterioration of the irrigation systems on which they were based.[1]

During the several millennia since irrigation began, it has spread throughout the world. By 1900, irrigation covered some 40 million hectares. Between 1900 and 1950, it expanded to 94 million hectares. Then soaring world demand for food led to an explosive increase, with irrigation covering 206 million hectares in 1978. (See Figure 8–1.) In 28 years, the irrigated area per person expanded from 0.037 hectares to 0.048 hectares, a gain of 28 percent.[2]

Million
Hectares

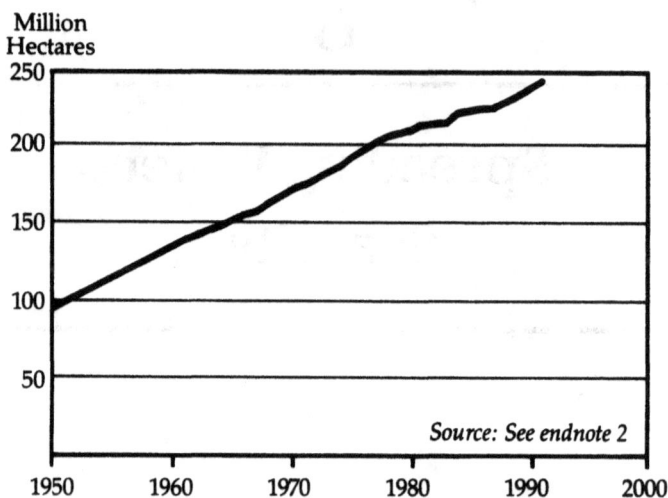

FIGURE 8-1. *World Irrigated Area, 1950–91*

The year 1978 marked the end of rapid growth. From then until 1991, the last year for which data are available, irrigated land expanded from 206 million hectares to 244 million. During this period, growth in irrigation fell behind that of population, and the irrigated area per person shrank to 0.045 hectares, a loss of 6 percent. (See Figure 8–2.)[3]

The 150 million hectares added to the world's irrigated area after mid-century involved the diversion of river water as well as the pumping of underground water. Since these both involve large capital commitments, irrigation was a major focus of public investments by national governments and international development agencies. In addition, farmers drilling wells on their own land contributed to these impressive gains.[4]

Hectares

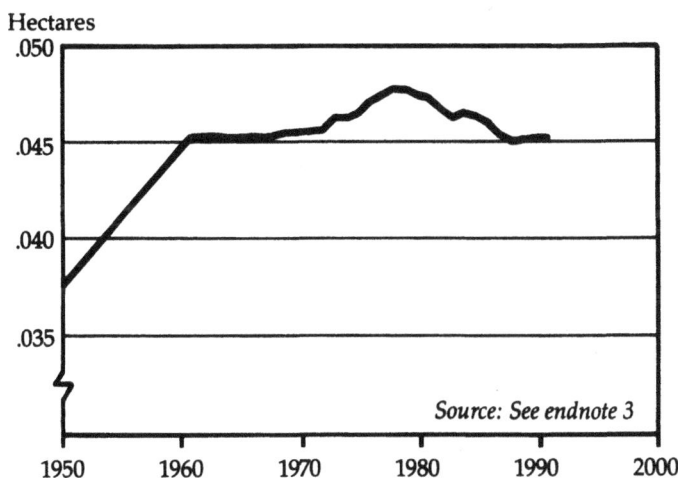

FIGURE 8-2. *World Irrigated Area Per Person, 1950–91*

The conditions conducive to irrigation from rivers are concentrated in Asia, which has some of the world's great rivers—the Indus, the Ganges, the Brahmaputra, the Chang Jiang (Yangtze), and the Huang He (Yellow). These originate at high elevations and traverse long distances, providing numerous opportunities for dams and the diversion of water onto the land in a network of gravity-fed canals and ditches. As a result, some two thirds of the world's irrigated area is in Asia.[5]

China and India lead the world, with 48 million and 43 million hectares of irrigated land, respectively. (See Table 8–1.) Growth in irrigated area in China between 1950 and 1980 was particularly impressive, increasing by an estimated 140 percent, well ahead of the global pace. This facilitated an increase in multiple cropping, among other things, from an average of 1.3 crops per hectare in 1950 to 1.5 in 1980.[6]

TABLE 8-1. *Net Irrigated Area, Top 20 Countries and World, 1990*

Country	Irrigated Area	Share of Cropland Irrigated
	(million hectares)	(percent)
China	47,837	50
India	43,050	27
Soviet Union	21,215	9
United States	20,891	11
Pakistan	16,500	81
Indonesia	7,600	37
Iran	5,750	38
Mexico	5,180	21
Thailand	4,300	19
Romania	3,216	14
Spain	3,370	17
Italy	3,120	26
Bangladesh	2,933	33
Japan	2,847	61
Afghanistan	2,760	4
Brazil	2,700	5
Egypt	2,607	100
Iraq	2,550	6
Turkey	2,370	9
Sudan	1,900	15
Total	202,696	19
Other	36,845	10
World	239,541	17

SOURCE: See endnote 6.

India's net irrigated area in 1950 was 21 million hectares, almost exactly the same as China's. Though growth was less rapid, the total nevertheless more than doubled. India's irrigated area is vast by international standards, but the number overstates the potential somewhat, since many of the earlier large river diversion projects were designed to protect against monsoon failures rather than to intensify production. The most rapid growth has occurred since the mid-sixties, following the introduction of high-yielding wheat and rice varieties that were both more responsive to water and more exacting in their demands.[7]

The former Soviet Union and the United States rank third and fourth, respectively, in irrigated area. U.S. irrigated area grew rapidly from 1950 to 1980, as did the irrigated area in the former Soviet Union. The Soviets looked to irrigation not only to help boost food production but also to minimize the wide swings in crop output that result from highly variable rainfall.[8]

Irrigation often holds the key to cropping intensity, especially in monsoonal climates, where the wet season is followed by several months with little or no rain. Where temperatures permit year-round cropping, as they often do where monsoons prevail, irrigation allows the production of two or three crops per year.

Since the early sixties, underground water development with wells drilled especially for irrigation has become relatively more important than the development of surface water. In India, in particular, the more profitable high-yielding varieties introduced in the mid-sixties led to heavy investments by farmers in their own wells, particularly in the Gangetic Plain. Similarly, much of the irrigation expansion in the United States since mid-century has been in the southern Great Plains, based on the use of underground water and large, center-pivot irrigation systems.[9]

For water efficiency, irrigation wells are invariably far superior to the large-scale river diversion projects relying on dams and networks of canals, simply because they enable farmers to control precisely the timing and amount of water applied to their fields. Indeed, the doubling of the wheat harvest in India between 1965 and 1972 depended in part on the spread of well irrigation.[10]

Unfortunately, not all the irrigation expansion since mid-century is sustainable. The growing demand for fresh water for all uses—industry and residences as well as irrigation—is exceeding river flow rates. As a result, some of the world's major rivers, such as the Amu Darya in Central Asia, now run dry before they reach the sea. Other major rivers, such as the Colorado in the United States and the Huang He in China, carry much less water to the sea than they once did.[11]

Elsewhere, water tables are being drawn down as pumping exceeds aquifer recharge. This drawdown is most dramatic when irrigation is based on fossil aquifers, which cannot be recharged. In the U.S. Southern Great Plains, farmers draw water from the Ogallala aquifer, a fossil reserve of underground water. Throughout the Texas panhandle, on the southern fringe of the Ogallala, where it is more shallow, many farmers have gone back to dryland farming as water supplies have been depleted. In Saudi Arabia, a heavily subsidized wheat production effort that relies on a fossil aquifer deep underground is being cut sharply in 1994 as fiscal stringencies dictate a reduction in government outlays. The cutback in subsidies, which support wheat prices at five times the world market level, will cut irrigated area and wheat production by nearly half in 1994.[12]

In the world's two major food-producing countries, the United States and China, there has been little growth in irrigation since 1980. In the United States, depressed commodity prices and rising pumping costs played a role. In late 1993, Dan Beard, the new Commissioner of the U.S. Bureau of Reclamation, outlined a major shift in irrigation policy when he said, "federally funded irrigation water supply projects will not be initiated in the future." He went on to discuss the need to "focus limited federal funding on increasing efficiency and remediating adverse impacts of existing projects."[13]

As early as 1986, the U.S. Department of Agriculture (USDA) reported that one fourth of the 21 million hectares of irrigated cropland was being watered by pulling down water tables, with the drop ranging from 6 inches to 4 feet per year. Although water mining is an option in the short run, in the long run withdrawals cannot exceed recharge.[14]

In China, there is evidence of deterioration in some community irrigation systems due to neglect arising from the shift to family-centered farming that began in 1978. Beyond this, irrigation in northern China is threatened by a growing scarcity of fresh water and the associated transfer to nonfarm uses. Under parts of the North China Plain in the region surrounding Beijing and Tianjin, the water table is dropping by 1–2 meters per year. Both industrial and residential claimants are taking water away from agriculture.[15]

Few realize how tight the water supply has become in China, particularly in the northern region. In late 1993, Chinese Minister of Water Resources Niu Maosheng said, "in rural areas over 82 million people find it difficult to procure water. In urban areas the shortages are even worse. More than 300 Chinese cities are short of water, and 100 of them are very short." The aquifer under Beijing has dropped from 5 meters below the surface in 1950 to 50 meters in 1993.[16]

There is also extensive overpumping in India. Although no comprehensive groundwater study comparable to the USDA survey exists for India, several states report that water tables are falling and that wells are going dry. In Tamil Nadu, a water-short state on the southeastern coast, the water table in some areas fell 25–30 meters during the seventies.[17]

A recent study shows that even in the Punjab, India's breadbasket, overpumping is pulling down the water table. As noted in Chapter 7, the introduction of the high-yielding, early-maturing wheats and rices in the sixties meant farmers could double-crop, with wheat in winter and rice in the summer. The combination of intensive irrigation and the heavy use of fertilizer on both crops dramatically boosted agricultural productivity, but it also led to overpumping and a decline in groundwater tables. In Ludhiana district, one of 12 in India's Punjab, where the water balance has been carefully studied, the water table is falling nearly 1 meter a year. A plan to use water more efficiently and to reduce the total amount pumped, which would reduce yields by some 8 percent, could stabilize the water table.[18]

For Asia, where more than half the world lives, construction sites for new dams are scarce and invariably costly to develop. With overpumping now so widespread, the potential for expanding well irrigation is also limited. Irrigation analyst David Seckler observes that "the major Asian countries are reaching the practical limits to expansion of irrigated land, even without environmental quality constraints."[19]

In some situations, where underground drainage is inadequate, problems are caused by rising—not falling—water tables. Water percolating downward can gradually raise the water table. If it reaches within a few feet of the surface, deep-rooted crops cannot develop properly in the waterlogged soil. If it rises to within a foot or less, the underground water begins to evaporate through the soil, leaving behind a surface film of salt. At some point, salt accumulates to levels that are toxic to plants, at first reducing yields and then eventually rendering the soil barren. Roughly one tenth of the world's irrigated area appears to be suffering from salinization serious enough to reduce yields. Another 30 percent may be moderately affected.[20]

One of the world's most environmentally disastrous irrigation projects is located in the former Soviet Union in the Central Asian republics surrounding the Aral Sea. Water from the Amu Darya and Syr Darya, which once emptied glacial melt from the mountains of northeastern Afghanistan and Kyrgyzstan into this vast geologic depression in Soviet Central Asia, now irrigates surrounding cropland. The Amu Darya disappears before it reaches the Aral Sea; the Syr Darya is a mere trickle when it arrives.[21]

The eventual result was the demise of the Aral Sea, a process that began in 1960 when planners in Moscow inaugurated the Aral Sea Project, an ambitious economic program to convert virtual wasteland into the cotton belt of the Soviet Union. Irrigated area doubled in less than a decade to nearly 7 million hectares, more than twice that of California.[22]

By Moscow's account, the early years of the project were a success. Production quotas for cotton and other commodities were met or exceeded year in and year out. The Aral Sea basin became the country's leading supplier of fresh produce, much as California is for the United States. Incomes climbed in the five republics that share the basin—Kazakhstan and Uzbekistan along the shores of the sea, and Kyrgyzstan, Tajikistan, and

Turkmenistan to the south in the drainage of the Amu
Darya and Syr Darya.

But the early high hopes for the project were short-
lived. With its sources nearly dry, sea level has dropped
some 32 meters in the last 30 years, reducing the Aral's
area by 40 percent and its volume by 66 percent. Rising
salt concentrations have destroyed all fish and the fishery that once yielded more than 40 million kilograms of
fish per year. If recent trends continue, the sea will
largely disappear within another decade or two, existing
only as a geographic memory.[23]

As the Aral Sea shrinks, it leaves behind a vast salt-
covered plain incapable of supporting plant life. Each
year, the wind sweeps up sand and an estimated 90 million tons of salt in blinding storms, depositing it across a
broad area, ranging from the farms of Belarus in the
northwest to Afghanistan in the southeast.[24]

The Aral Sea basin may be experiencing some of the
worst salinization in the world. Nikita Glazovsky, a
prominent Russian geographer, reports that the share of
irrigated land that is moderately to heavily salted ranges
from 35 percent in Tajikistan to 80 percent in Turkmenistan. For the entire basin, it is 60 percent.[25]

Using cotton yields as an indicator, the productivity
of land in the Aral region has fallen nearly 15 percent
since peaking in 1979. Unless the waterlogging and salting are reversed quickly, yields will continue to fall until
eventually the land becomes sterile and is abandoned.
For the 32 million people who live in the Aral Sea basin,
with its irrigation-based economy, the economic effects
of environmental decline are all too obvious.[26]

On every continent, the diversion of irrigation water
to nonfarm uses is now becoming commonplace as
water needs of cities and industries multiply. When this
happens in states like Texas or Colorado, the land typi-

cally goes back to dryland farming. When irrigation water is diverted to cities in more arid regions, such as Arizona or southern California, the land goes back to desert. In parts of Arizona where irrigation water has been diverted to Tucson or Phoenix, agriculture has disappeared. In North China, satisfying Beijing's water needs means that land that only a few years ago was irrigated has now reverted to rainfed agriculture.[27]

Over the longer term, expanding irrigated area may depend almost as much on efficiency gains as on supply expansion. Many governments have subsidized irrigation water, making it unrealistically cheap and leading to its wasteful use. In some countries, such as the United States, this provides low-priced water for farmers from large, government-funded irrigation projects, most notably those in California. In India, heavy electricity subsidies that cover 84 percent of the cost to farmers who have their own wells encourage excessive water use.[28]

New irrigation technologies and practices that boost the efficiency of water use are evolving rapidly. For example, switching from continuous to intermittent flooding of rice, a practice that keeps the soil saturated but does not require it to be constantly under water, can reduce water use per ton of rice produced by up to 40 percent. Drip irrigation, a technique perfected and widely used in Israel in fruit and vegetable production, yields even greater savings.[29]

In summary, the slower growth in irrigated area since 1978 is characteristic of the new water era. Many countries will continue to expand their irrigated areas; others will have difficulty even maintaining existing irrigation as water is diverted to nonfarm uses. It now seems unlikely that a rapid irrigation growth trend can be reestablished.

Depletion of fossil aquifers, falling water tables elsewhere, growing competition for water from nonfarm sources, the silting of irrigation reservoirs, and the abandonment of severely salted irrigated land all suggest that future net gains in irrigation will be modest and that they will rest heavily on gains in water efficiency. It also seems likely that the decline in irrigated area per person under way since 1978 will continue for as far as we can see into the future, making it ever more difficult to boost per capita food production.

9

The Fertilizer
Falloff

When German chemist Justus von Liebig demonstrated
in 1847 that all the nutrients that plants removed from
the soil could be returned in mineral form, he set the
stage for an explosion in world food production a century later. At the time of his discovery, the frontiers of
agricultural settlement were still being pushed back.
The U.S. Homestead Act, designed to encourage settlement of the West, was still to come. With many opportunities to expand the cultivated area, there was little
pressure to increase soil fertility and raise land productivity.[1]

Several trends converged a century later to launch the
steep climb in world fertilizer use. By mid-century, the
frontiers had largely disappeared. And almost overnight,
population growth shifted from low gear to high. Faced

with record growth in world food demand and little new land to plow, farmers responded by pouring on fertilizer to raise land productivity, boosting their grain yields from 1.1 tons to 2.4 tons per hectare within four decades.[2]

Thus, fertilizer has been at the center of advances in world food output during the last four decades. In a sense, other technologies have been designed to facilitate its use. Irrigation, for example, permits the heavy use of fertilizer, resulting in high yields. Similarly, the new varieties have high yields precisely because they are much more responsive to fertilizer than traditional ones.

The trend in world fertilizer use since mid-century divides into three distinct eras: From 1950 to 1984, annual use climbed from 14 million tons to 126 million tons, expanding ninefold or nearly 7 percent a year—one of the more predictable global economic trends. From 1984 to 1989, growth continued, climbing to 146 million tons, but at a much slower pace—roughly 3 percent a year. Then from 1989 until 1993, fertilizer use dropped each year, falling back to 126 million tons in 1993. (See Figure 9-1.)[3]

The new trend in fertilizer use has two components. One is agronomic: the declining response of grain yields to additional fertilizer at higher levels of use. The second is economic, specifically the decision by governments in major food-producing countries to reduce or eliminate fertilizer subsidies. The drop in the agronomic response to additional fertilizer slowed the rise in use in the late eighties, bringing it to a near standstill. But the actual decline in use since 1989 is largely the result of reducing subsidies in key food-producing countries such as the former Soviet Union, India, and, most recently, China.[4]

As grainland area per person has shrunk since mid-

Million
Tons

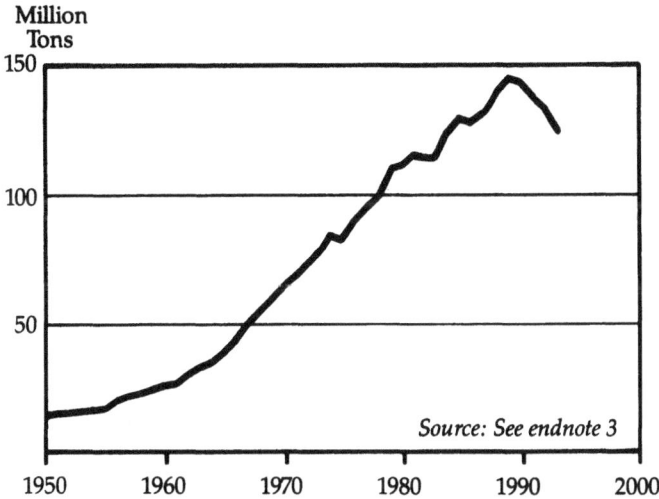

FIGURE 9-1. *World Fertilizer Use, 1950–93*

century, fertilizer use per person climbed from 6 kilograms to the historical high reached in 1989 of 28 kilograms per person. (See Figure 9–2.) As long as production could be expanded by substituting fertilizer for land, farmers could easily stay ahead of population. But this period has ended, at least for now. In a sense, the trends in Figure 9–2 highlight the overriding dilemma facing humanity—how to maintain rapid growth in grain production now that the use of additional fertilizer is having little effect on production where yields are high.[5]

The shrinkage of cropland per person was not the only trend driving the growth in fertilizer use. Two others—urbanization, a demographic trend, and the growth in dependence on imported grain in many countries, an economic trend—also played a part. Both disrupted the

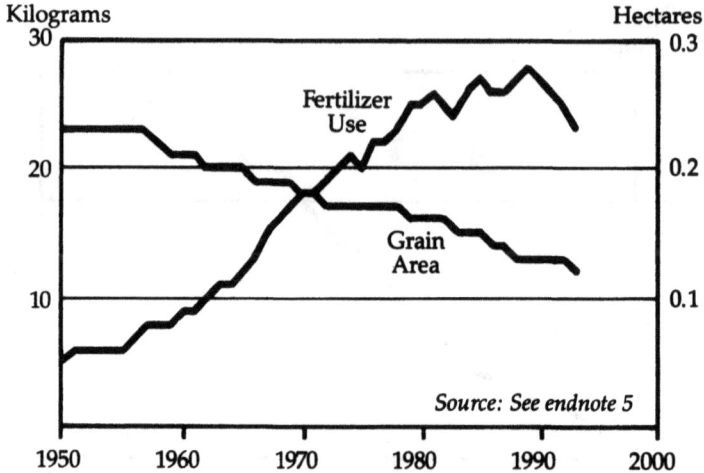

FIGURE 9-2. *World Grain Harvested Area and Fertilizer Use Per Person, 1950–93*

natural nutrient cycle. As people moved into cities, the nutrient recycling that occurs in rural areas when human wastes are returned to the land becomes more difficult, and in some cases prohibitively costly.[6]

As more and more countries turn to imported grain, the nutrient cycle is further disrupted. The United States, which exported close to 100 million tons of grain a year during the eighties, suffered a heavy loss of soil nutrients. The nutrients in the wheat from Kansas and the corn from Iowa were ending up in the sewage discharges of St. Petersburg, Cairo, Lagos, Caracas, and Tokyo. In order to maintain soil fertility, there was no alternative but to replace the lost nutrients with mineral sources.[7]

One consequence of these trends was a steady increase in the intensity of fertilizer use throughout the world. In 1950, fertilizer use per hectare of grainland totalled some 24 kilograms. When it peaked in 1989, it was 211 kilograms. Since then it has fallen some 12 percent, to roughly 186 kilograms per hectare. (See Figure 9–3.)[8]

Fertilizer use per person has also reversed in recent years, dropping from the historical high of 28 kilograms in 1989 to less than 23 kilograms in 1993. This drop of 19 percent helps explain why grain production per person has fallen in recent years.[9]

Fertilizers have three key nutrients: nitrogen, phosphorus, and potassium. At the global level, nitrogen is by far the most important, accounting for roughly half of total fertilizer use, with the remainder divided rather evenly between phosphorus and potassium. In addition, fertilizers today incorporate minute amounts of minor

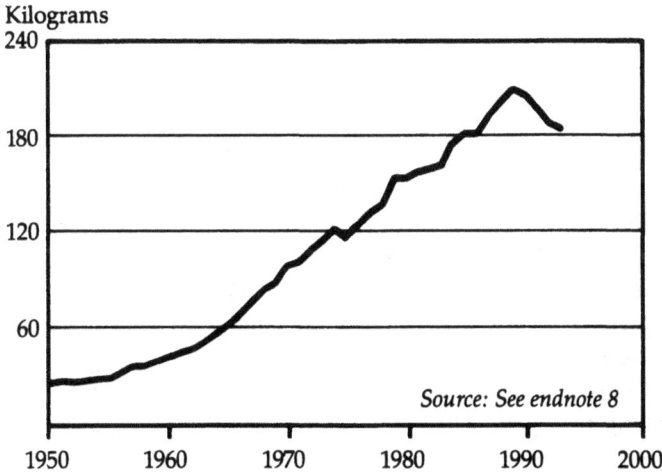

Kilograms

Source: See endnote 8

FIGURE 9-3. *World Fertilizer Use Per Hectare of Grainland, 1950–93*

nutrients, such as magnesium, sulfur, or boron, with the formulation reflecting local soil conditions and nutrient needs.[10]

For the supplies of phosphate and potash, the world is indebted to geologists who have discovered underground deposits. For nitrogen, credit goes to two German chemists, Fritz Haber and Carl Bosch, who, beginning in World War I, devised a means of fixing atmospheric nitrogen in a form that could be applied to the soil and assimilated by plants.[11]

Since mid-century, the steadily expanding use of fertilizer has been the engine driving the growth in world food production. Every country that has achieved high levels of land productivity has done so with the heavy use of fertilizer. Some individual farmers have achieved high levels without chemicals, relying entirely on local organic sources. (For example, in East Asian countries, particularly Japan, Korea, and China, urban sewage is used by farmers immediately surrounding the city in an agriculturally intensive green belt of vegetable growing.) But no country has been able to do so.[12]

Within the big four countries, trends in fertilizer use contrast sharply. In Moscow, central planners once saw the use of fertilizer as a way of dramatically boosting food production. Forced to turn to the outside world for imports, they steadily increased fertilizer use from the early sixties onward until, by the early eighties, they had overtaken the United States to become the world leader. (See Figure 9–4.)[13]

This situation, however, was short-lived, because by 1988 the Soviet leaders were adopting economic reforms that included removing the fertilizer subsidy. In effect, they let fertilizer prices rise to the world market level, which was far higher than that fixed by the central

Million
Tons

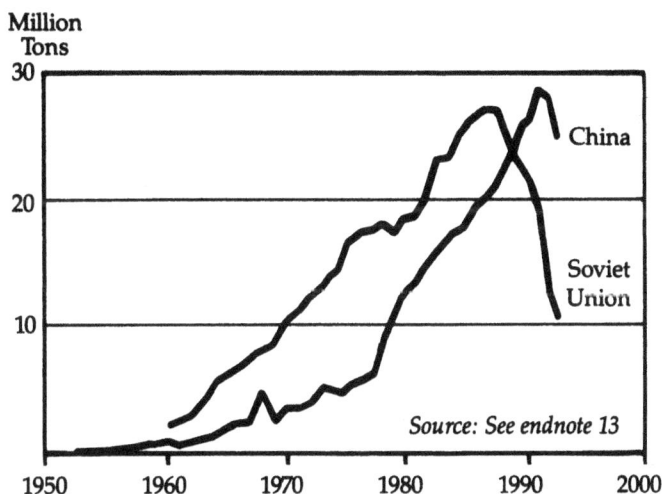

FIGURE 9-4. *Fertilizer Use in China and the Soviet Union, 1950–93*

planners. As a result, Soviet fertilizer use was cut in half within five years, dropping from 27 million tons to 13 million.[14]

This contrasts with the situation in China, where economic reforms launched in 1978 to convert to a market economy quickly tripled fertilizer use. At that time China's farmers were using just under 9 million tons of fertilizer. By 1993, this had climbed to nearly 29 million tons, surpassing both the former Soviet Union and the United States.[15]

Of the major food producers, the United States was the first in which fertilizer use levelled off. (See Figure 9–5.) After a rapid increase from 1950 through 1980, growth came to an abrupt halt. Since then usage has actually fallen as grain area has dropped somewhat,

Million
Tons

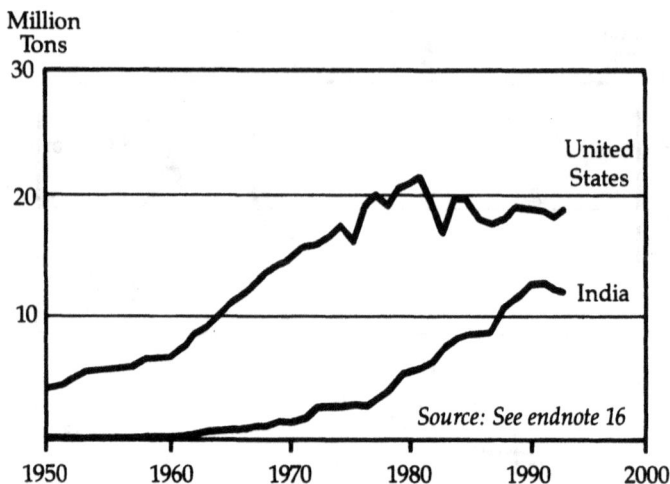

FIGURE 9-5. *Fertilizer Use in the United States and India, 1950–93*

leading to lower fertilizer use in the early nineties than a decade earlier. Some of the decline is due to more sophisticated tests that enable farmers to match fertilizer applications more precisely to plant needs, thus eliminating excessive use.[16]

In India, fertilizer use climbed rapidly in the late eighties, largely as a result of heavy government subsidies. By the early nineties, though, opposition to this fiscal drain led to a reduction in subsidies and much slower growth in use. Without subsidies, future growth in fertilizer use is also likely to be slower.[17]

Of the big four grain producers, China has the smallest area of cropland—roughly two thirds as much as the United States and India and scarcely half that of the former Soviet Union. Nonetheless, it has taken the lead in fertilizer use because it has the world's largest irrigated area, a key to the productive use of fertilizer.[18]

In addition to the decline in use, the early nineties have witnessed another landmark development: in 1992, fertilizer use in developing countries surpassed that in industrial countries for the first time. A ranking of countries in terms of fertilizer use in 1993 puts China at the top with 29 million tons, the United States second with 18 million tons, the former Soviet Union third with 13 million tons, and India fourth with 12 million tons. This heavy use of fertilizer worldwide underlines the difficulty of expanding food output that faces all countries, but particularly developing ones that are expecting large additions to their populations.[19]

The formula of using more fertilizer to raise land productivity was phenomenally successful from 1950 to 1984, when fertilizer use climbed to a new high nearly every year. During this time, each additional ton of fertilizer applied boosted grain output 9 tons. (See Table 9-1.)[20]

But 1984 was the last year in which a large increase in fertilizer use led to a comparable gain in world grain output. During the next five years farmers continued to use more fertilizer, but their crops did not respond much. Each additional ton of fertilizer raised grain output by less than 2 tons. By 1989, the United States, Western Europe, the former Soviet Union, and much of Eastern Asia, including Japan and China, had raised yields to a point where adding more fertilizer had little effect on production.

Given such a weak response, applying more fertilizer was clearly not a money-making proposition. Farmers' reaction, both predictable and rational, was to use less. Between 1989 and 1993, they cut fertilizer use some 12

TABLE 9-1. *World Grain Production and Fertilizer Use,*
1950–93

Year	Grain Production	Incre- ment	Fertilizer Use[1]	Incre- ment	Incremental Grain/ Fertilizer Response[1]
	(million tons)				(ratio)
1950	631		14		
1984	1,649	1,018	126	112	9.1
1989	1,685	36	146	20	1.8
1993	1,682	– 3	120	– 20	—[2]

[1]Assumes that all fertilizer is used for grain; although this is obviously not the case, it provides a broad picture of the changing response. [2]Incremental ratio cannot be calculated because fertilizer use declined.

SOURCE: See endnote 20.

percent. Even excluding the precipitous drop in the former Soviet Union following economic reforms that removed subsidies, usage elsewhere dropped by 3 percent.[21]

This decline in the crop response to fertilizer use was not a surprise to everyone. In a 1987 analysis of trends in Indonesia, Cornell economists Duane Chapman and Randy Barker noted that "while one kilogram of fertilizer nutrients probably led to a yield increase of 10 kilograms of unmilled rice in 1972, this ratio has fallen to about one to five at present."[22]

Seeing fertilizers as the key to expanding food output, many governments decided in the seventies and eighties to subsidize their use. Today, efforts to rationalize economic activity, often encouraged by the World Bank, have eliminated this practice in many developing countries. Indeed, while the relationship between grain and fertilizer prices has fluctuated, the dominant economic influence on use in the last few years appears to be the reduction of fertilizer subsidies.[23]

Further reductions in fertilizer use could come as a result of negotiations under the General Agreement on Tariffs and Trade completed at the end of 1993. To the extent that producer support prices for commodities encourage fertilizer use beyond what world market prices would justify, their reduction could lower fertilizer use. This effect is likely to be relatively small, however, compared with the reduction in direct fertilizer subsidies.[24]

In the short term, fertilizer use will likely decline slightly in 1994 as it bottoms out prior to resuming gradual growth in 1995. Over the long term, both irrigation expansion and transportation improvements are likely to boost use. In parts of Africa, improved transport will effectively lower the cost of fertilizer to farmers. If grain prices rise in the years ahead, they will encourage investments in both land reclamation and irrigation. And these, in turn, will raise fertilizer use.

But unless someone can design new strains of wheat, corn, and rice that are much more responsive to fertilizers than those now available, future gains in grain output from rising use are likely to be modest. It is difficult to visualize any conditions evolving that will lead to rapid, sustained growth in fertilizer use similar to the one that occurred from 1950 to 1984. If large gains in food output cannot be achieved from using more fertilizer, where will they come from?

10

Struggling to Raise Yields

The ancients calculated yield as the ratio of grain harvested to that sown. For them, the scarce resource was the seed itself. Today's farmers have little opportunity to add fertile land to the world's cultivated area. For them, land productivity is the key indicator. Indeed, the food prospect for the next four decades depends almost entirely on raising land productivity.

Countries that have doubled or tripled the productivity of their cropland since mid-century are the rule, not the exception. But with many of the world's farmers already using advanced yield-raising technologies, further gains in land productivity will not come easily. Some sense of the future potential for doing so can be gleaned from looking at yield trends for wheat, rice, and corn in countries with the highest yields—for example, corn in the United States, wheat in the United Kingdom, and rice in Japan.

Yields of corn, a cereal widely used for feed and food, are highest in the United States, which accounts for 40 percent of the world harvest. Data for U.S. corn yields from 1866 to 1993 divide into three distinct periods. (See Figure 10–1.) During the seven decades from the Civil War to World War II, yields were essentially unchanged, averaging about 1.6 tons per hectare. From 1940 to 1985, the average yield jumped more than fourfold, reaching a phenomenal 7.4 tons per hectare. But in the eight years since then, the rise has slowed to a near standstill.[1]

A similar situation exists for wheat in the United Kingdom, which has the highest yield of any major wheat-producing country. (See Figure 10–2.) From 1884 until 1940, yields were remarkably stable. From

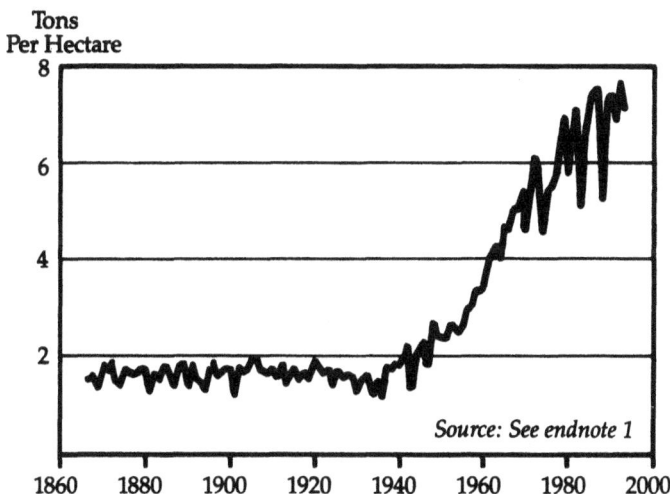

Tons
Per Hectare

Source: See endnote 1

FIGURE 10-1. *U.S. Corn Yield, 1866–1993*

1940 until 1985, they more than tripled. But since 1985, U.K. wheat yields have fluctuated around 7 tons per hectare, showing little evidence of a continuing rapid rise.[2]

The rise in wheat yields in other parts of Europe with similar growing conditions is slowing as yields approach the U.K. level. Among these are Germany and France, the latter a wheat exporter. The rise is also slowing in the United States and China, the world's two largest wheat producers. Since wheat in these two countries is grown in largely low-rainfall regions, the slowdown is occurring at yield levels one third to one half those in Western Europe. In China, the big jump in wheat production came immediately after the economic reforms in 1978, as yields climbed 81 percent from 1977 to 1984. During the following nine years, however, they rose only 16 percent.[3]

For rice, the key to understanding the yield potential is Japan, a country that has worked hard to raise its rice yields for more than a century. After this extended climb, the rise in Japan came to a halt in 1984. Since then, yields have actually fallen slightly. (See Figure 10–3.) Yields in China, the world's largest rice producer, now approach Japan's and have been stable since 1990. In India, however, the second-ranking rice producer, the yield rise is slowing at a much lower level. In Japan and China, 99 and 93 percent, respectively, of the rice is irrigated; in India, the figure is only 44 percent, making it far more difficult to achieve high yields. The yield rise has also slowed in other major rice-producing countries, including Indonesia, Pakistan, and the Philippines.[4]

A similar trend exists in other high-technology rice-producing countries, such as South Korea, Taiwan, and

Tons
Per Hectare

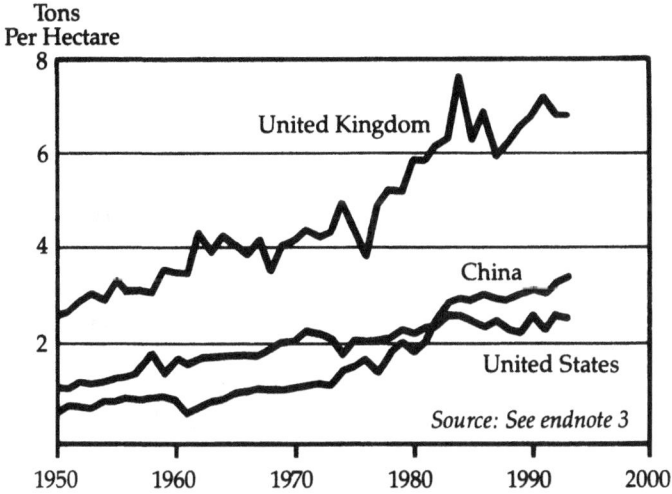

FIGURE 10-2. *Wheat Yields, United Kingdom, China,*
and United States, 1950–93

Tons
Per Hectare

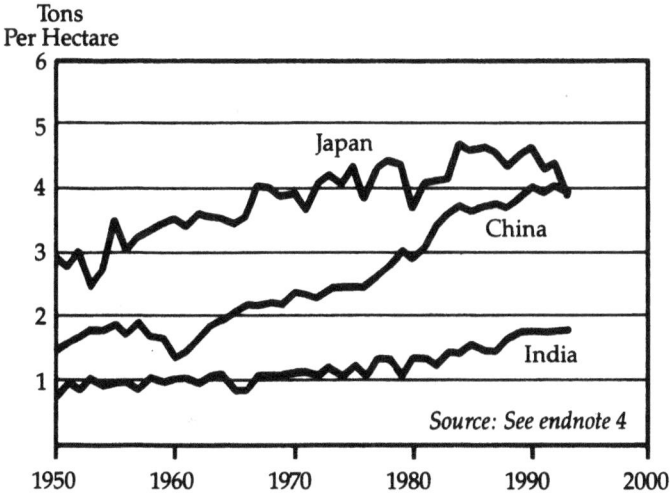

FIGURE 10-3. *Rice Yields, Japan, China, and India, 1950–93*

Italy. In each case, once rice yields pass 4 tons per hectare, they rise quite slowly or level off, suggesting that
dramatically boosting rice yields above this level may
require new technological advances. Agricultural economists Duane Chapman and Randy Barker of Cornell
University point out that "the genetic yield potential of
rice has not increased significantly since the release of
the high yielding varieties in 1966."[5]

These recent slowdowns in the rise in grain yields are
sobering. Between 1950 and 1984, the world grain yield
per hectare more than doubled, rising 118 percent or
2.3 percent a year. But from 1984 until 1993, yields rose
only 1 percent a year. (See Figure 10–4.) Since 1990, a
year of exceptional growing conditions worldwide, grain
yield per hectare has actually declined slightly.[6]

This slowdown is a worldwide phenomenon afflicting
industrial and developing countries alike, largely be-

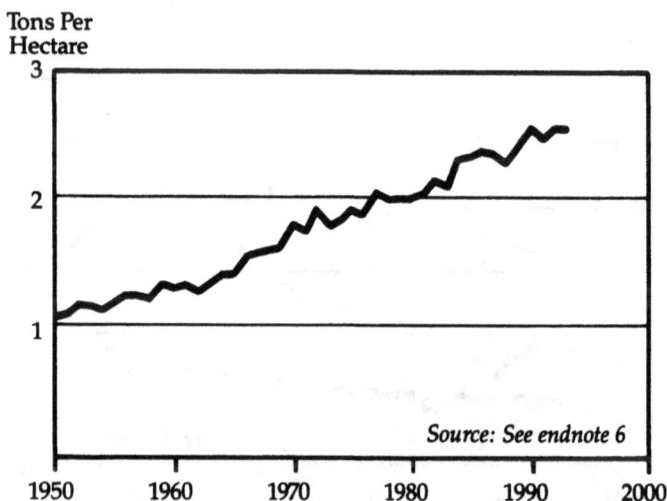

FIGURE 10-4. *World Grain Yield, 1950–93*

cause all countries now draw on the same international pool of technology. Unfortunately, the slower yield increase raises questions about the earth's carrying capacity and, specifically, about the ability of the world's farmers to feed an ever growing population.

The systematic application of science to agriculture has permitted a regular increase in yields for nearly two generations, making it difficult to imagine a situation in which yields will not continue their steady rise. Nonetheless, a study published in 1993 observes that rice yields on experiment stations in Asia have been stagnant now for many years. In the absence of any new yield breakthroughs, a future of slowly rising or static yields may now be in prospect for many rice-growing countries.[7]

Also of concern, many Asian rice farmers who have boosted output by continuously cropping rice with two or three harvests per year are experiencing a decline in yields. Scientists testing this cropping practice report that efforts to intensify agricultural production by continuously cropping rice with two or even three crops per year have actually led to a decline in yields on test plots in the Philippines, India, Bangladesh, and Thailand.[8]

At the International Rice Research Institute in the Philippines, plots producing three crops a year from 1963 to 1993 now show a decline in yields of more than 1 percent annually. After 89 consecutive rice crops, with inputs held constant, yields are slowly declining. Apparently, the continuous flooding of the plots alters soil microbial activity, the physical structure of the soil, and its chemistry in ways that adversely affect yields. The only viable alternative is to replace one of the rice crops in the three-crop annual cycle with one that does not need to be flooded.[9]

As early as 1986, Robert Herdt, senior economist at the Rockefeller Foundation, observed that the backlog of unused technology available to farmers appeared to be dwindling. He noted that in some farming communities, crop yields on the best farms approached those on experimental plots.[10]

Rising grain yield per hectare, like any other biological growth process in a finite environment, must eventually give way to physical constraints. Where farmers supply all the nutrients and water that advanced varieties can use, cereal yields may now be pushing against various physiological limits, such as nutrient absorption capacity or photosynthetic efficiency.

For those who remember biology class experiments that involved measuring the growth in a petri dish of an algae population with an unlimited food supply, this deceleration will not come as a surprise. With algae, it is the buildup of waste that eventually checks growth, bringing it to a halt. For grain with unlimited fertilizer supplies and abundant soil moisture, the plant's physiological limits will ultimately restrain the rise in yield.

Grain production per hectare is a process that relies on photosynthesis to convert solar energy into biochemical energy. Albeit modified by human intervention, it is—like all natural processes—subject to the limits of nature. These boundaries have been pushed back with great success during the last several decades, but that does not mean this can continue indefinitely.

More and more analysts are beginning to realize that the trend of steadily rising yields over recent decades may not continue in the future. Identifying the need for raising the genetic yield potential of a crop and being able to do so are not the same. In the United States, for example, corn yields have more than tripled since mid-century. Soybean yields, meanwhile, have gone up by roughly half, or only one sixth as much as corn. Even though the crops are produced by the same farmers on the same land, farmers have not been able to raise soybean yields much at all even though a bushel of soybeans is worth more than twice as much as a bushel of corn. Despite a powerful economic incentive to raise soybean yields dramatically, no one has been able to do so. (See Figure 10–5.)[11]

Contrary to popular opinion, biotechnology is not an agricultural panacea that will end hunger. Perhaps the best assessment of the potential contribution of biotechnology is one by Donald Duvick, former director of research at the Pioneer Seed Company. He points out the two main ways to use biotechnology. One is to map the genetic structure of crops, such as wheat, rice, and corn;

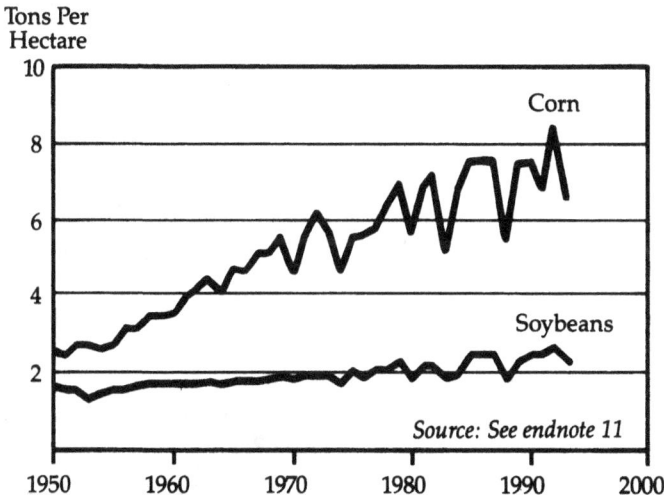

FIGURE 10-5. *U.S. Corn and Soybean Yields, 1950–93*

linking specific genes to specific traits can be an invaluable aid to plant breeders. The other, a unique contribution of biotechnology, is the transfer of germplasm from one species to another.[12]

Biotechnology can be used to breed resistance to diseases and insects or to raise the genetic yield potential of the crop. The new technology is likely to make its earliest contributions in the former, either in reducing the need for pesticides or in lowering crop losses. In either case, these are likely to be local solutions, since plant diseases and insects tend to be location-specific.[13]

In the all-important area of raising the genetic yield potential of major crops, nothing is in prospect. Nor would it be wise to count on any major contribution on this front simply because so much of this potential has been exploited using conventional plant breeding techniques.

Despite the astounding gains in molecular biology, which provides the foundation for harnessing the potential of biotechnology, expansion of food output through this new technique thus far has been limited. Duvick notes that although we have had great hopes for contributions from biotechnology for the past 20 years, the projected date when this new research tool would make a meaningful contribution to plant breeding has "receded annually, staying always five to ten years in the future."[14]

In summary, no prospective breakthroughs in plant breeding are likely to lead to dramatic jumps in food output similar to the hybridization of corn or the dwarfing of wheat and rice. Minor incremental gains in raising the genetic yield potential of major crops will continue, but many of these will be localized, the result of breeding efforts tailored to specific local conditions.

The higher the genetic yield potential of a crop rises, the harder it is to find new opportunities for boosting it further. As more and more of the world's farmers use varieties with the highest genetic yield potential, it becomes more difficult to achieve rapid gains in world food output.

In some ways, the dramatic yield gains of the last generation or so are like the gains in life expectancy. Between 1950 and 1990, average life expectancy worldwide increased from 46 to 64 years, a gain of 18 years or 39 percent. This relatively easy advance was rooted in broad-based gains in public health, immunization, and nutritional improvement. Boosting life expectancy another 39 percent—to 89 years—over the next four decades will, however, be exceedingly difficult. Gains in human life expectancy are also limited by genetic potential, a potential that eventually imposes limits on the extension of life expectancy, even with the best of diets and health care.[15]

In addition to some of the more obvious influences on yields, such as inherent soil fertility and, with rice, the availability of irrigation, latitude also plays a role. Countries near the equator—where days are shorter—have lower rice yields than those in the middle latitudes. Japan and China have higher yields than India, for example. And yields in Indonesia and the Philippines, both astride the equator, are among the lowest of the major rice-producing countries.[16]

Failure to recognize the recent slowdown in yield gains and the reasons for it can generate overly optimistic projections. In a study issued in late 1993 entitled *The World Food Outlook*, World Bank economists Donald O. Mitchell and Merlinda D. Ingco project world food supply and demand to 2010, assuming that the linear growth in grain yield per hectare between 1960 and 1990 will more or less continue until 2010. This makes for a rather hopeful set of projections. Unfortunately, there is no scientific foundation for this assumption, given the dramatic slowdown in the rise of grain yield per hectare during the late eighties and early nineties. This analysis misses the abrupt deceleration in the rise in yields that has occurred since 1984. Indeed, from 1990 to 1993, the first three years in the Bank's 20-year projection period, worldwide grain yield per hectare actually declined.[17]

Environmental degradation is also undoubtedly slowing the rise in yields. (See Chapter 11.) The yield effect of the earlier rapid rise in fertilizer use may have obscured the negative effects of soil erosion, air pollution, waterlogging and salting, and other forms of degradation. But where fertilizer use is no longer rising, these effects may become more visible.

Some have hypothesized that a rise in cereal prices would stimulate investment in agriculture, restoring rapid growth in world food production. Higher prices will raise investment, but the scale may be limited. For example, investing in more irrigation pumps and wells where water tables are already falling will only hasten the depletion of the aquifer. Similarly, investing in more fertilizer in situations where there is no meaningful yield response will not have much effect on output.[18]

Perhaps the best test of the price hypothesis has occurred in Japan, where the government supports rice prices at six times the world market level. Boosting rice yields in Japan is extraordinarily profitable. Yet try as they might, Japan's farmers—scientifically literate, hard-working, and with access to cheap credit—have not raised rice yields at all over the last decade. They are searching everywhere for new yield-raising technologies, but neither the agricultural experimental stations nor the seed companies and the fertilizer manufacturers have much to offer.

Few countries that have doubled or tripled grain yields over the last few decades can expect to match that record in the future with existing technologies. Most have either already achieved the easy dramatic rises or lack the natural conditions needed to do so.

In semiarid Africa, for example, where yields have risen little, the prospects for sharply increasing output during the next four decades are no better than they were for Australia's farmers, who boosted wheat yields by less than half between 1950 and 1990. Every country that has multiplied its yields has relied heavily on the same basic combination of water (either from relatively generous rainfall or from irrigation), fertilizer, and grain varieties that are highly responsive to fertilizer. Those that lack water are severely handicapped in efforts to dramatically raise yields.[19]

A further troubling element is the declining public support for agricultural research both within individual countries and at the international level. Research played a major role in developing the fertilizer-responsive grain varieties that have helped double and triple yields. It also helps maintain yield gains in the face of new insect, disease, and environmental threats.

Declining investment has recently extended to the international research centers, such as the International Rice Research Institute in the Philippines and the International Maize and Wheat Improvement Center in Mexico, both part of the network known as the Consultative Group on International Agricultural Research (CGIAR). Overall CGIAR funding dropped in 1993 and again in 1994 (see Figure 10–6); this decline was largely driven by a sharp drop in the U.S. core contribution—from $43 million in 1992 to $28 million in 1994, a cut of 35 percent.[20]

Many food projections, such as those by World Bank economists Mitchell and Ingco, assume the generation of new technologies at past rates, but this can no longer be taken for granted. If research funding continues to fall, maintaining even past yield gains could become a challenge.[21]

In summary, there are innumerable small opportunities for raising land productivity, many of them locally unique. But opportunities for large production jumps are now confined to a few countries that have had ill-conceived policies or have failed to concentrate on agri-

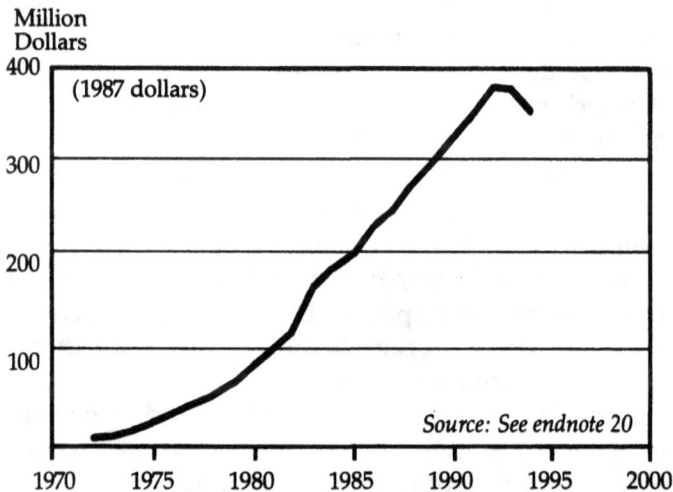

FIGURE 10–6. *Funding for International Agricultural Research Institutes, 1972–94**

* Includes the 17 institutes in the Consultative Group on International Agricultural Research.

cultural development, such as Myanmar or Argentina. And increased funding for agricultural research could enlarge the supply of technologies that help make yield maintenance and increased yield possible in developing nations. But the present identifiable technologies for further raising yields in agriculturally advanced countries are relatively small.

11

Environmental Deductions

During the seventies, scientists at Mauna Loa Observatory in Hawaii, who measure the atmospheric concentration of carbon dioxide, began analyzing the dust content of their air samples. They learned that the fine dust in their samples was soil particles from the Asian mainland. The peak dust content comes each year in March, April, and May, a time that coincides with a period of strong winds, low rainfall, and plowing in the semiarid regions of North Asia. Within a matter of days, the scientists at Mauna Loa could tell when spring plowing started in North China.[1]

The deposit of soil in the Pacific Ocean from the croplands of China is but one of thousands of examples of how the earth's agricultural support systems are being damaged. The environmental degradation of the planet, in its many forms, affects all sectors of the global economy, but none as much as the food sector. Losses stem from damaged and eroded soils, air pollution, waterlogging and salting of irrigated land, depleted aquifers, and increasing ultraviolet radiation. Some come from agriculture itself and the burden it puts on the land. Others come from outside—from the energy, chemical, and transport sectors.

A pattern of population growth, deforestation, and soil degradation has repeated itself around the world in recent decades. World Bank energy analyst and ecologist Kenneth Newcombe has described how complex, interrelated systems unravel through several stages. His model, based on fieldwork in Ethiopia, portrays a cascading decline in biological and economic productivity triggered by loss of tree cover. As people seek new agricultural land, natural forests retreat before the plow. Without trees, mineral nutrients are no longer recycled from deep soil layers. As this nutrient cycle is breached, soil fertility begins to decline.[2]

As populations grow, demand for wood rises. Village families who suddenly lack wood burn crop residues and animal dung to heat their homes and to cook. That interrupts another nutrient cycle—it removes crop residues and dung from fields, which degrades soil structure and leaves the land yet more vulnerable to erosion. Once nearby stands of trees are gone, this process accelerates. The steady loss of nutrients and organic matter from croplands limits crop yields and the ability of pastures to support livestock.[3]

Eventually, cow dung becomes the main fuel source in villages and thus the main cash crop from nearby farms. Pervasive topsoil depletion leaves farmers vulnerable to total crop failure during even routine dry seasons. Food and fuel prices rise rapidly. A massive exodus from rural areas begins, often triggered by drought that formerly could have been tolerated. Famine is widespread; peasants' lack of purchasing power is compounded by absolute shortages of food at any price.[4]

Land degradation is taking a heavy toll on food production, particularly in the drylands that account for 41 percent of the earth's land area. In the early stages the costs of land degradation show up as lower land productivity. But if the process continues unarrested, it eventually creates wasteland, destroying the soil as well as the vegetation. Using data for 1990, a U.N. assessment of the earth's dryland regions estimated that the degradation of irrigated cropland, rainfed cropland, and rangeland now costs the world more than $42 billion a year in lost crop and livestock output, a sum equal to the value of the U.S. grain harvest. Damage to rainfed and irrigated cropland together account for $19 billion of this total. (See Table 11–1.)[5]

Lost productivity on Africa's rainfed cropland, largely from soil erosion, has reduced the annual harvest by an estimated $1.9 billion, roughly the same as Tanzania's gross national product. In Asia, the losses are larger mainly because of the waterlogging and salting of irrigated land: for irrigated land, rainfed cropland, and rangeland, they total nearly $21 billion a year—by far the largest of any geographic region. Deterioration in humid regions of the world, which includes the U.S. Corn Belt and Europe's rich agricultural regions, also takes a heavy toll, though no one has calculated it.[6]

From erosion, the world's farmers are losing billions of tons of topsoil from their cropland each year. In 1985, the United States lost an estimated 1.6 billion tons of topsoil from cropland in excess of new soil formation.

TABLE 11-1. *Annual Losses in Crop Production from Land Degradation in Dryland Regions*

Continent	Rainfed Cropland	Irrigated Land
	(billion dollars)	
Africa	1.9	0.5
Asia	4.6	8.0
Australia	0.5	0.1
Europe	0.4	0.5
North America	0.4	1.5
South America	0.2	0.3
Total[1]	8.2	10.8

SOURCE: See endnote 5.

With one hectare-inch of topsoil weighing 400 tons, this figure can be visualized as one inch being lost from 4 million hectares. A compilation of more than a dozen U.S. studies analyzing the effect of erosion on land productivity found that losing an inch of topsoil reduces corn and wheat yields an average of 6 percent. With nature requiring centuries to form an inch of topsoil, current losses are irreversible when time horizons are measured in decades or generations.[7]

The World Bank, citing studies for Costa Rica, Malawi, Mali, and Mexico, concludes that the gradual losses of agricultural productivity from soil erosion now translate into annual losses in farm output equal to 0.5–1.5 percent of those countries' gross domestic product. Although estimates of the economic effects vary widely, there can be no question that soil erosion is taking a heavy toll on the earth's productivity. In the extreme, the effects can be seen in the countless aban-

doned villages in countries such as Ethiopia, where there
is not enough soil left to support even subsistence-level
agriculture. And in the former Soviet Union, land degradation, mostly from erosion, helped convert some 20
percent of the area in grain in 1977 to soil-conserving
forage crops, alternate-year fallowing, or wasteland by
1993. Lacking anything like the U.S. Conservation Reserve Program, many countries have simply continued
to farm highly erodible land until it turns into wasteland.[8]

With irrigated land, the principal threat to productivity is waterlogging and salinity. As noted in Chapter 8,
roughly one tenth of the world's irrigated area appears
to be suffering from salinization serious enough to reduce yields, with another 30 percent moderately affected and additional amounts suffering from waterlogging.[9]

The reservoirs and canals that store and supply irrigation water suffer from a different problem: sedimentation. Silt carried by river water collects in reservoirs behind dams and fills in the storage basins, thereby
reducing the capacities of the dams and even destroying
them. A global analysis by the World Bank put losses to
reservoirs' storage capacity from sedimentation at an average annual rate of 1 percent. The cost of replacement
for that annual loss of capacity is "modestly" estimated
by the Bank at $6 billion a year. "The magnitude of
capacity already lost is very large," says the study.[10]

Some countries have suffered particularly large losses.
The Roseires Reservoir in Sudan, which supplies water
for irrigation during the dry season, lost one third of its
capacity due to a buildup of silt during just nine years
beginning in the late seventies. The loss was attributed
to deforestation along the watersheds of the Blue Nile.

The Ethiopian government had moved tens of thousands of farmers into the watershed by clearing 10,000 hectares of remnant virgin forests. The silt also clogged irrigation canals and encouraged the growth of aquatic weeds. The weed-choked canals became breeding grounds for waterborne diseases, all of which were on the increase.[11]

The Anchicaya dam project in the Colombian Amazon lost 80 percent of its storage capacity in only 12 years due to siltation during the sixties. The Ambuklao dam in the Philippines had its operational life expectancy of 75 years reduced by more than half for the same reason. In addition to the cost of replacing or losing the dams, the trapping of annual soil deposits behind dam barriers deprives fields downstream of seasonal nutrient replenishments. By one estimate, from 25 to 75 percent of the sediments normally carried downstream can be lost. Despite a history of sedimentation problems, however, new dams continue to be built on some of the rivers with the highest sediment loads.[12]

Air pollution, now almost as pervasive as soil erosion, is also lowering agricultural productivity. In some parts of the world, it takes an even greater toll. In Sweden, where it is moderate compared with some industrial countries, yields of the more sensitive food crops such as potatoes and oats are suffering. Air pollution costs an estimated 350,000 tons of grain per year in lost output, 6 percent of the annual harvest. In heavily industrialized Czechoslovakia, with some of the world's worst pollution, scientists estimate an annual harvest loss of all crops from air pollution at a value equal to 1.3 million tons of wheat.[13]

For the United States, where some 70 monitoring stations indicate crop-damaging concentrations of ground-level ozone in every part of the country, the financial loss is far greater. A joint study by the Environmental Protection Agency and the U.S. Department of Agriculture indicates that crops are affected in varying degrees. Overall, the study estimates that the annual crop harvest in the United States has been lowered by at least 5 percent because of air pollution and perhaps as much as 10 percent. Applying these proportions to the annual harvest, with a market value of around $70 billion, yields a loss of $3.5 billion to $7 billion. Worldwide, given coal-burning countries such as China, India, and those of Eastern Europe, losses must be several times this amount.[14]

In vegetation, ground-level ozone—the most broadly destructive form of air pollution—causes damage to the photosynthetic mechanism and to leaves, and it provokes changes in growth rates, yields, and quality. Ozone also lowers plants' resistance threshold to stress factors. Because of its toxicity, ozone is now regarded as the worst air pollutant. It is joined by a catalog of others, however, from sulfur and nitrogen oxides to hydrocarbons.[15]

Only a handful of studies have measured the effect on crops of increased ultraviolet (UV) radiation resulting from depletion of the stratospheric ozone layer. Results thus far obtained, however, have revealed a significant threat to food production. In a six-year study of the Essex soybean, economically the leading soybean in the U.S. mid-Atlantic states, yields fell 20–25 percent under increased UV radiation. Some other varieties of soybeans may be less susceptible, and through breeding it might be possible to reduce the damage. Those changes, however, would require years of work and heavy research investment merely to maintain yields.[16]

With rice, only preliminary information is available. Of the approximately 200 different cultivars of rice now screened for UV sensitivity, between one half and one third have been found to be very sensitive. Some 10 percent, however, seem to be very resistant, which raises the possibility of breeding around the problem. If that becomes necessary and focuses on the narrow part of the genetic spectrum of rice that is oriented toward UV resistance, then breeding for other desirable traits will be negatively affected.[17]

Studies on corn in the early eighties, before instrumentation was as effective as it now is, showed large reductions in corn yield from UV light as well. A repeat of these studies with state-of-the-art techniques would help clarify more precisely the consequences for corn production of stratospheric ozone depletion. Many of the effects on plants of exposure to increased ultraviolet radiation are only beginning to unfold. Preliminary results from two multiyear research projects by the Commonwealth Scientific and Industrial Research Organization in Australia and the International Rice Research Institute in the Philippines show that both wheat and rice suffer impaired photosynthesis and stunted growth.[18]

For the most carefully researched crops, like soybeans, a 15-percent reduction in stratospheric ozone results in roughly a 15-percent reduction in yield. With seafood, studies have also shown essentially a one-to-one ratio between ozone depletion and marine productivity. Research from the major Antarctic biological stations has shown that at current levels, ultraviolet radiation from the sun harms phytoplankton cellular processes, including reproduction, DNA integrity, and survival. If phytoplankton abundance or health are affected, that would ripple through the entire marine food chain—with unpredictable effects.[19]

Because different species vary in their response to UV radiation, ozone depletion can change species composition or the abundance, size, distribution, or nutritional value of primary producers. Studies between 1987 and 1991 found that the photosynthesis and production of phytoplankton have diminished by 6–12 percent in the water around Antarctica because of increased ultraviolet radiation, reducing the food available to fish and other higher species. At the surface, where most productivity takes place, photosynthesis has been reduced by as much as 20 percent. With losses of stratospheric ozone projected to continue for several decades, even if chlorofluorocarbon manufacturing is halted soon, the potential effects on food production deserve far more monitoring and research.[20]

Farmers, who have always had to deal with the vagaries of weather, now also face the unsettling prospect of climate change. Agriculture has evolved over a 10,000-year period of remarkable climatic stability. Any major departure from those conditions will cause enormous hardship and require incalculable investments during the adjustment.

The most advanced global climate models indicate that a doubling of the preindustrial level of carbon dioxide (CO_2), or the equivalent when the effect of other greenhouse gases is taken into account, would raise the global temperature by between 1.5 and 4.5 degrees Celsius (2.7–8.1 degrees Fahrenheit). If the world continues on a business-as-usual path, the most recent projections show this occurring as early as 2030, a point much closer to us in time than the end of World War II.[21]

These projected temperature rises are global averages, but scientists now agree that the increases would not be spread evenly; they would be far greater in the middle and higher latitudes, and also greater over land than over the ocean. Temperatures near the equator are expected to change very little as the earth warms, while rises in the higher latitudes could easily be twice the average projected for the globe as a whole. Most of the world's food is produced in the northern hemisphere, and most of it within the middle and higher latitudes. Relatively little is produced near the equator, where climate change would be least.[22]

Though they remain sketchy, meteorological models suggest that two of the world's major food-producing regions—the North American agricultural heartland and the principal grain-growing regions of the former Soviet Union—are likely to experience a decline in soil moisture during the summer growing season as a result of higher temperatures and increased evaporation.[23]

If the warming unfolds as the models indicate it will, the land in the western U.S. Great Plains that now produces wheat would revert to grassland. The western U.S. Corn Belt would become semiarid, with wheat or other drought-tolerant grains that yield 2.5 tons per hectare replacing corn, which yields 7 or more tons. Land values would drop in anticipation of the shift to less-productive crops. On the plus side, as temperatures increase, the winter wheat belt would shift northward, with winter wheat yielding 2.5 tons per hectare replacing spring wheat that yields just under 2 tons per hectare. A longer growing season would also permit a northward extension of spring wheat production in areas such as Alberta, Canada, thus increasing overall cultivated area.[24]

One of the highest costs facing world agriculture

would be the adjustment of irrigation and drainage systems. As the warming proceeds and rainfall patterns change, both these systems would become redundant in some situations and inadequate in others. According to one analysis, adjusting irrigation systems alone could require an investment of some $200 billion worldwide.[25]

Over the longer term, sea level rise caused by global warming would flood coastal farmland and threaten many low-lying and heavily populated areas, such as the Nile delta and large parts of Bangladesh, with more frequent storm-surge inundation. Expanding oceans could claim large pieces of low-lying riceland in the river deltas and floodplains of Asia. Salinization of coastal aquifers would increase, reducing sources of irrigation water.[26]

Another variable related to climate change that will influence future levels of food production is the rising level of carbon dioxide in the atmosphere, although the effect is hard to gauge. Under laboratory conditions, two of the three grains that account for the bulk of the world grain harvest—wheat and rice—respond positively to enhanced CO_2 levels in the environment. Corn, which has a somewhat different metabolic pathway for fixing carbon, is not responsive to additional atmospheric carbon dioxide.[27]

Much of the uncertainty about the effect of CO_2 centers on the extent to which other environmental conditions are constraining yield increases. In situations where moisture, nutrients, soil condition, temperature, or solar intensity are limiting yield increases, additional CO_2 in the atmosphere will not have any effect. To cite a parallel example, applying fertilizer to soils that are arid has little effect on yields simply because there is not enough moisture to increase the yields even if an unlimited supply of nutrients is available.[28]

Accurately assessing the effects of environmental degradation on future food production trends would be a complex process even if data on such things as the extent of soil erosion and the effects of exposure to increased ultraviolet radiation were readily available. Without such data, it is virtually impossible. But we do know that various forms of degradation, such as soil erosion or the salting of irrigated land, have a cumulative effect over time.

IV

Looking
Ahead

12

Carrying Capacity: The Big Four

With the rise in grain yields now slowing and the yield of oceanic fisheries and rangelands unlikely to increase much if at all, there is an urgent need for national assessments of carrying capacity. Otherwise, there is a real risk that countries will blindly overrun their ability to grow food, developing massive deficits that will collectively exceed the world's exportable supplies. Recent data showing the level at which the rise in grain yield per hectare is slowing in the most agriculturally advanced countries provide governments with the reference points needed to estimate the population carrying capacity of their croplands.[1]

Because we have neither the time nor the space to project the population carrying capacity for all countries, we have selected two groups. The first consists of the four largest food-producing nations—the United States, China, the former Soviet Union, and India. Together these four account for well over half the world's food production and nearly half its population. The second group of nine populous countries, containing one sixth of world population, is covered in the next chapter.[2]

These projections cover the next four decades, from 1990 to 2030. It is easier to do projections for shorter periods, but the time horizons of both population and climate policy call for a longer view. Although 2030 seems rather remote, it is closer than 1950, a year many policymakers can easily remember.

The population figures used in this exercise are the medium-level projections of the Center for International Research of the U.S. Bureau of the Census. They are similar to the more widely used medium-level U.N. projections, but are updated more frequently and are thus more current.[3]

Several assumptions underpin our grain supply and demand projections. One, designed to simplify the demand projections and highlight the effect of population growth, is that future growth in demand generated by rising incomes will not play a major role. Accordingly, no allowance is made for income-generated growth in demand for any country. The result for countries such as China, where incomes are rising rapidly, is some exceedingly conservative projections of demand.

Another key assumption is that there will be no dramatic technological breakthroughs that will lead to quantum jumps in world food output comparable to those associated with the discovery of fertilizer, the hybridization of corn, or the development of the high-yielding dwarf wheats and rices. Although this may seem unreasonable, the last major technological advance in raising crop yields—the hybridization of corn—occurred more than 70 years ago. In other words, 70 years have passed without a major breakthrough, despite record investments in agricultural research. Nonetheless, there will be innumerable yield-raising technological advances or adaptations that will boost output modestly in local areas. The third assumption is economic—namely, no change in grain prices. In many ways, these are business-as-usual projections.[4]

The grain production projections here attempt to incorporate the emerging constraints on growth in output, such as the shrinking backlog of unused yield-raising technologies, the diminishing yield response of cereals to the use of additional fertilizer, the need to reduce excessive irrigation pumping to restore a balance between pumping and aquifer recharge, the effects on agriculture of social disintegration and political instability, and the effect on production of various forms of environmental degradation, such as soil erosion, waterlogging and salinity, air pollution, increased ultraviolet radiation, and rising levels of greenhouse gases.

Projections of grain output are typically made by assuming a certain area and a rate of growth of yield per hectare and then simply extending it into the future. Recent studies by the World Bank and the U.N. Food and Agriculture Organization (FAO) use historical yield gains from 1960 to 1990 and simply extrapolate these into the future as linear trends. The rationale for doing this, according to World Bank analysts, is that the past is the only guide we have to the future. The weakness of this approach is that it misses the dramatic slowdown in the rise in yields that has occurred in the late eighties and early nineties and fails to take into account the tendency of all biological growth processes in a finite environment to eventually follow an S-shaped curve.[5]

If, for instance, the rising use of fertilizer in a country has recently crossed the yield-response threshold, beyond which there is no meaningful response, it makes no sense to project the long-term historical trend into the future. Similarly, if an aquifer is nearing depletion, historical irrigation pumping rates cannot simply be extended into the future. And the same can be said about the world fish catch: extrapolating the trend from 1950 to 1990 into the future would yield results that would bear little relationship to reality.

With this in mind, we subjectively evaluate for each country the various inputs that have contributed to gains in production in the last four decades and then look at the broad array of factors likely to affect output during the next four. For example, is irrigated area likely to increase as much in absolute terms in the future as it has in the past? Has the growth in fertilizer use come to a halt, at least for the time being, or is it likely to resume rapid growth for some time? Are there any forms of environmental degradation, such as soil erosion or the salting of irrigated land, that are likely to affect production trends markedly?

In looking at future production potential, reference is frequently made to the countries that have already achieved some of the highest yields. For rice-growing countries, for instance, yields in Japan serve as the likely upper limit that other countries will be able to achieve in the absence of a dramatic technological breakthrough. Similarly, for semiarid countries in Africa, the advanced agriculture of Australia offers a useful reference point for assessing long-term yield potentials. China's potential can be set beside that of the United States, which appears to be roughly a decade ahead on the fertilizer use curve. In this important respect, the techniques here differ from those used in recent projections by FAO and the World Bank.

Differences between our projections and the two official ones are partly the result of contrasting time horizons. Since they look only at 1990–2010, they cannot show nearly as fully the growing gap between continuous population growth and the finite land and water resources available to produce food.

The assumptions and thinking behind the projections for each country are summarized in the text so that those who wish to replace our assumptions with their own can easily do so. (No effort is made in the country-by-country projections to balance global grain imports and exports; the huge excess of imports over exports yielded by these projections is discussed in Chapter 14.) There is not anything sacred about these projections. They are not carved in stone, but are intended to stimulate thought about the changing food/population balance and to encourage others to come up with their own forecasts.

We begin this exercise with the United States, source of half the world's grain exports. On the demand side, grain consumption is projected to increase apace with population. Assuming no gain in per capita consumption, the projected addition of 95 million people (38 percent), which includes growth from natural increase and immigration, would raise consumption from 214 million tons in 1990 to 295 million tons in 2030.[6]

On the supply side, grain production in the United States has been essentially flat for the last decade, with the highly erodible land removed from production roughly offsetting modest yield gains. With the addition of 95 million people, satisfying the demand for residential building, industrial sites, parking lots, shopping centers, schools, and recreation areas will claim large areas of cropland. With water continuously being diverted from agriculture to satisfy growing urban and industrial needs, and with the inevitable downward adjustments to eliminate overpumping, the net irrigated area is unlikely to expand much.

The question then becomes, How much can land productivity be raised in a country that already has some of the world's highest yields? A review of the last four decades shows that the yield gain per decade, which totalled 45 percent in the fifties and 43 percent in the sixties, dropped to 20 percent in the seventies and to a mere 10 percent in the eighties. (See Table 12–1.)[7]

One reason for the slower rise in yields during the seventies and eighties, but particularly during the latter, is that crops are no longer responding appreciably to

TABLE 12-1. *United States: Grain Yield Per Hectare by Decade, 1950–90*

Decade[1]	Annual Yield Per Hectare	Increase by Decade
	(metric tons)	(percent)
1950	1.65	
1959–61	2.40	+ 45
1969–71	3.43	+ 43
1979–81	4.13	+ 20
1989–91	4.56	+ 10

[1]Three-year averages are used to minimize the effect of weather fluctuations.

SOURCE: See endnote 7.

additional fertilizer, which is already being applied at a high rate. As noted earlier in *Full House*, unless new crop varieties can be developed that will respond to ever greater amounts of fertilizer, future increases in production from this source will be minimal during the four decades under projection.

Could the United States find itself in the not too distant future in a situation similar to Japan over the past decade, unable to raise yields at all? Perhaps, but in projecting U.S. grain production over the next four decades, we assume a continuing rise in yields, albeit at a slightly slower rate than during the eighties, averaging 7 percent a decade or roughly 30 percent through 2030.

Another assumption is that the U.S. cropland losses to nonfarm uses associated with the addition of 95 million people will be offset by the return to production of cropland idled under commodity supply management programs and at least part of the land now under the Conservation Reserve Program. In fact, in 1994 all grainland previously idled under the commodity programs has been released for planting. Some of the land under the Conservation Reserve Program could be farmed on a sustainable basis with some adjustment in farming practices, such as the adoption of crop rotations or minimum tillage. On balance, however, there is not likely to be much change in the cropland area during the next four decades.[8]

The boost in total output of 30 percent between 1990 and 2030 would increase the harvest from 290 million tons in 1990 to 377 million tons in 2030. (See Table 12-2.) The anticipated addition to output of 87 million tons over 40 years compares with 157 million tons that were added since 1950. If these projections materialize, the exportable surplus of grain would be raised slightly

TABLE 12-2. *Grain Production, Consumption, and Net Trade in "Big Four" Countries, 1950 and 1990, With Projections to 2030[1]*

Country	Grain Production	Grain Consumption	Net Trade
	(million tons)		
United States			
1950	133	121	+12
1990	290	214	+76
2030	377	295	+82
China			
1950	109	109	0
1990	329	335	−6
2030	263	479	−216
India			
1950	57	55	+2
1990	158	158	0
2030	222	267	−45
Former Soviet Union			
1950	79	80	−1
1990	182	219	−37
2030	237	262	−25

[1]To stabilize the base for the projections, the data shown for 1990 are actually a three-year average for 1989–91.

SOURCE: See endnote 9.

from 76 million tons to 82 million tons. This follows a drop of actual exports between 1980 and 1990 from 121 million to 76 million tons.[9]

Next we look at China, a country that now grows even more grain than the United States. In 1990, China produced 329 million tons of grain and consumed 335 million tons, with the difference covered by imports of 6 million tons. Allowing only for the population increase of 490 million projected for this period, China's demand for grain would increase from 335 million tons in 1990 to 479 million tons in 2030.[10]

On the supply side, we are projecting a decline of one fifth in China's grain production during the next 40 years. This will initially surprise many, particularly those familiar with the dramatic rise in grain production in China since the 1978 reforms. Yet when countries that are already densely populated industrialize rapidly, the loss of cropland eventually overrides the rise in land productivity, leading to an absolute decline in production.

The precedent for this can be seen in each of the three countries in East Asia where this has happened. The result for Japan was that between 1960, when it peaked, and 1992, grain production dropped 33 percent or 1 percent a year. (Using Japan's 1993 weather-depressed harvest number here would distort the trend.) For South Korea, the peak in production came in 1977, dropping 31 percent over the next 16 years, or 1.9 percent a year. For Taiwan, where the peak also occurred in 1977, output dropped 19 percent by 1993, or 1.2 percent a year.[11]

In each case, as production was dropping, demand was climbing steadily, fueled by continuing population growth and soaring per capita incomes. The net effect was that by 1993, Japan was importing 77 percent of its grain, South Korea 68 percent, and Taiwan 74 percent. At 27 million tons, Japan is today the world's leading importer of grain.[12]

The per capita grain area in China in 1990 was 0.08 hectares per person, midway between the 0.06 that Japan had in 1950 and the 0.10 of both South Korea and Taiwan. Inherent land productivity in China is somewhat less than in the other three countries because of extensive dryland farming in the west and north.

Throughout the northern half of the country, virtually all available fresh water is spoken for, which means that additional water for industrial or residential uses will likely come at the expense of agriculture.[13]

The conditions in China are very similar to those in the three countries just cited. Rapid industrialization in recent years has taken its toll on cropland as grain area has dropped from 90.8 million hectares in 1990 to an estimated 87.4 million in 1994. This annual drop of 850,000 hectares, or 1 percent—remarkably similar to the cropland losses experienced by Japan, South Korea, and Taiwan—is likely to endure for the foreseeable future if rapid industrialization continues.[14]

Beyond the claims on cropland of industrialization, the living space needs for 490 million additional people during the next four decades, some 12 million per year, will also claim millions of hectares of farmland. Even if China launches a concerted national effort to preserve cropland, it is doubtful it could be any more successful than Japan, which has long had some of the strongest agricultural land protection laws of any country. In the immediate vicinity of Tokyo, where land prices are among the highest in the world, every tiny plot of rice land is vigorously protected from development.[15]

What are the prospects that China can sustain a rise in land productivity sufficiently rapid that it would more than offset the loss of cropland? None of the three countries just discussed was able to do it—not even Japan, where the rice support price is six times the world market level. Another reference point is the United States. In expanding fertilizer use, China appears to be roughly a decade behind the United States, where usage peaked in the early eighties at 22 million tons. China's annual fertilizer use peaked in 1993 at 29 million tons and dropped slightly in 1994, partly because of a drop in fertilizer subsidies and partly because of the shrinking cropland area.[16]

If the loss of grainland continues at the rate of the last four years, then the grain production decline that began in Japan in the sixties and in South Korea and Taiwan in the late seventies could start in China in the nineties. Indeed, it is quite possible that the harvests of the last four years—coming in rather consistently around 340 million tons each year—represent a production plateau that will be followed by a gradual decline during the next 40 years. Given the drops in output in Japan, South Korea, and Taiwan, it may be optimistic to assume that China can limit its decline to 20 percent over 40 years.[17]

If China's consumption needs increase to 479 million tons by 2030 as a result of population growth and if production drops 20 percent, the deficit will total 216 million tons—more than total world grain exports today. Imported grain as a share of consumption for China in 2030 would be 45 percent—still far below that of Japan, South Korea, and Taiwan.[18]

If we make an exception to one of our basic assumptions and consider the effect of rising income on grain consumption per person in China, assuming that it would increase from roughly 300 kilograms at present to 400 kilograms, the current level of consumption in Taiwan, this would add another 162 million tons of demand by 2030, pushing China's total consumption to a staggering 641 million tons. With production at 263 million tons, this would yield a deficit of 378 million tons.

The Chinese themselves have apparently been making similar calculations. Professor Zhou Guangzhao, head of the Chinese Academy of Sciences, observes that if the nation continues to squander its farmland and water resources in a breakneck effort to industrialize, "then China will have to import 400 million tons of grain from the world market. And I am afraid, in that case, that all of the grain output of the United States could not meet China's needs."[19]

Of the big four countries, India faces the largest population growth during the next four decades. Allowing for no improvements in diet, the projected gain of 590 million (69 percent) would boost grain consumption from 158 million to 267 million tons.

On the supply side, India nearly tripled its grain harvest between 1950 and 1990, no small feat for a developing country. Although the rise in yields has slowed in recent years, we assume that unrealized potential in India will enable it to achieve a 40-percent gain in production during the next 40 years, more than the 30-percent projected for the United States. Unfortunately, it is becoming much more difficult to expand food production in India. The grainland area that peaked in 1983 at 107 million hectares has since fallen to 102 million, a decline of 5 percent in 10 years. With the projected addition of 590 million people, the nonfarm claims on both cropland and water will be heavy. In a country where overpumping is already widespread, satisfying the residential needs for water of the additional population will come in part at the expense of irrigation. Against this backdrop, it comes as no surprise that India's grainland area is shrinking, and that it is likely to continue to do so as its population climbs toward 1.44 billion in 2030.[20]

It may be optimistic to project a growth in grain output in India at close to 1 percent per year, matching the global rate of growth from 1984 to 1993, given the cropland losses in prospect. Nonetheless, if it succeeds, India would boost its harvest from 158 million tons to 222 million tons. Achieving this will not be easy because some of the existing production is based on the unsustainable use of land and water. If it happens, India would still need to import 45 million tons of grain in 2030.

For this exercise, we have retained the former Soviet Union as a single unit in order to simplify the projections. Allowing for a 33-percent projected growth in population, most of it in the Asian republics, and no rise in per capita grain consumption, the consumption of grain in the former Soviet Union would increase from 219 million tons in 1990 to 291 million tons in 2030, a number that we need to adjust downward for reasons explained below.

The potential for expanding production in the former Soviet Union is limited by relatively low rainfall, harsh winters, and a short growing season. Like the United States, the former Soviet Union more than doubled grain production from mid-century to 1980. And, as in the United States, growth in production has slowed since then. A combination of soil erosion and soil compaction, the latter from using the world's heaviest tractors and farm equipment, has lowered the inherent productivity of Soviet soils. Irrigated land, most of it in the Aral Sea basin, is suffering from some of the worst waterlogging and salting found anywhere. As noted earlier, land productivity in the basin, measured by the yield of cotton, the principal crop, has declined on average 1 percent a year for nearly 15 years.[21]

In contrast to China, where agricultural reforms led to enormous increases in fertilizer use and dramatic gains in land productivity, reforms in the former Soviet Union effectively eliminated heavy fertilizer and food subsidies. As a result, fertilizer use fell by nearly half from 1988 to 1993 and grain fed to livestock has dropped from the high of 151 million tons in 1990 to 131 million in 1993, a fall of 13 percent. While the agricultural reforms in China dramatically boosted fertilizer use, in the Soviet Union they reduced it, largely because use was excessive and uneconomical.[22]

There is general agreement among agricultural analysts that Soviet economic reforms will do more to reduce the inefficient use of feedgrains and storage losses than they will to boost output. For this reason, we depart from our baseline assumption and reduce grain consumption per person 10 percent by 2030 to allow for gains in efficiency that are already under way. In effect, 10-percent less grain production (262 million tons) will be needed to satisfy the same level of consumption.

Many argue that, with economic reforms, Soviet grain yields could approach those of the United States, but this is not an appropriate comparison. With its northerly location, Soviet agriculture exists in a much more hostile environment, one more comparable to Canada, where wheat yields are only marginally higher. Thus we project growth in grain production during the next four decades at only 30 percent, since even this would mean pushing wheat yields well above those now prevailing in Canada. If demand increases to 262 million tons as a result of population growth, and if production increases to 237 million tons as projected, net imports would drop from 37 million tons in 1990 to 25 million tons in 2030.

The net effect of these projections for the "big four" is an enormous growth in demand for imported grain and a decline in grain available for export. In 1990, these four countries collectively exported 76 million tons of grain and imported 43 million tons. By 2030, they would be exporting 82 million tons of grain and importing 286 million tons, a net import deficit of 204 million tons. (See Chapter 14 for a discussion of this imbalance.)

In this exercise, we have tried to be very explicit about the assumptions and estimates used for each country so that the reader can substitute assumptions as desired to examine alternative scenarios. As noted earlier, the purpose of this exercise is not to argue unyieldingly for any particular assumption or projection, but simply to try and give a sense of how rapidly things are changing on the food front. And of how different the food prospect is now from what it appeared to be even a few years ago.

13

Carrying Capacity: The Next Nine

After the "big four" countries, nine other populous countries, containing some 900 million people, are individually large enough to affect the world food balance measurably. Four of these are in Asia (Bangladesh, Indonesia, Iran, and Pakistan), three in Africa (Egypt, Ethiopia, and Nigeria), and two in Latin America (Brazil and Mexico).

Pakistan, Iran, and Egypt have several things in common and can be discussed as a group. Each faces massive increases in population by 2030, with Egypt projected to more than double, Pakistan to nearly triple, and Iran to more than triple. Each has tripled its grain harvest over the last four decades. And all three depend heavily on irrigation.[1]

In Egypt, where it rarely rains, agriculture exists only because of water from the Nile. In Pakistan, only slightly less arid than Egypt, some four fifths of all cropland is irrigated. Both countries face severe water constraints on the expansion of grain output. Egypt has no prospect of getting more water from the Nile, and it could get less if upstream countries, especially Ethiopia, decide to take more.[2]

For Pakistan, Egypt, and Iran, we project grain production to increase by 50, 60, and 120 percent, respectively, over the next four decades. (See Table 13–1.) For Pakistan, progress is stymied by the extensive waterlogging and salting of its irrigated land, which is at least partly responsible for the decline in rice yield per hectare of roughly 1 percent a year during the last decade. Assuming that Pakistan can and will reverse the decline in rice yields, we estimate production growth during the next four decades at 9 million tons, only slightly below the 13 million tons of the last 40 years.[3]

Egypt has one of the smallest potentials for increasing production, both because its yields are already high by international standards and because water supply limits the expansion of its cultivated area. Nonetheless, the increment projected during the next four decades of 7 million tons is equal to the gain of the last four.

For Iran, where 38 percent of the land is irrigated and where yields are still relatively low, the increase is estimated at 14 million tons, up from the 8 million tons of the last 40 years. Iran is one of a relatively small number of countries outside Africa that have not systematically created the economic policies that would encourage the wholesale modernization of agriculture. Accordingly, it still has more unrealized production potential than many other countries do. Like Pakistan, however, Iran faces extensive waterlogging and salting of its irrigated land.[4]

These assumptions on future production trends for

TABLE 13-1. *Grain Production, Consumption, and Net Trade in Nine Populous Countries, 1950 and 1990, With Projections to 2030*[1]

Country	Grain Production	Grain Consumption	Net Trade
	(million tons)		
Bangladesh			
1950	8	8	0
1990	19	20	−1
2030	34	43	−9
Indonesia			
1950	12	12	0
1990	34	37	−3
2030	48	60	−12
Iran			
1950	4	4	0
1990	12	18	−6
2030	26	58	−32
Pakistan			
1950	6	6	0
1990	19	20	−1
2030	28	54	−26

each of the three countries combined with the projections of future demand generated by population growth show that by 2030 each nation will be a major importer. Pakistan, which imported barely 1 million tons in 1990, would need to bring in 26 million tons in 2030. Iran and Egypt would have to buy 32 and 21 million tons, respectively, continuing a trend in rising imports in both countries that has been under way for some years.

An environmental assessment for Pakistan undertaken with the assistance of IUCN–the World Conservation Union noted that the nation's population is projected to exceed 400 million by 2050. The report

TABLE 13-1. *(Continued)*

Country	Grain Production	Grain Consumption	Net Trade
		(million tons)	
Egypt			
1950	4	5	−1
1990	11	19	−8
2030	18	39	−21
Ethiopia and Eritrea			
1950	3	3	0
1990	5	6	−1
2030	9	18	−9
Nigeria			
1950	6	6	0
1990	9	9	0
2030	14	29	−15
Brazil[2]			
1950	10	11	−1
1990	37	43	−6
2030	67	71	−4
Mexico			
1950	4	4	0
1990	21	27	−6
2030	29	48	−19

[1]To stabilize the base for the projections, the data shown for 1990 are actually a three-year average for 1989–91.   [2]Projections for Brazil assume a rise in grain prices.

SOURCE: See endnote 3.

pointed out that while Pakistan might somehow accommodate an increase from its current 121 million to 200 million, it could not go much beyond that. If it remains on the trajectory toward 400 million Pakistanis, it "will become an international charity case—like Haiti, Ethiopia, Sudan, and Bangladesh—dependent on the good will of others, with no realistic opportunity to improve the lot of its people and no expectations other than the continual decline of living standards for the vast bulk of them." This description of Pakistan's prospects if it continues with a business-as-usual population policy applies equally well to many other countries with similar rates of population growth.[5]

The two other Asian countries in our analysis—Indonesia and Bangladesh—are both rice cultures, heavily dependent on rice as a staple food. In Indonesia, where rice yields have nearly tripled and are the highest for any equatorial country, the prospects for increasing production by more than 40 percent over the next four decades do not appear good. This increase would mean an additional 14 million tons of grain production, substantially less than the 22-million-ton increment from 1950 to 1990. Both the limited response of available rice varieties to additional fertilizer and the conversion of rice land to nonfarm uses as industrialization accelerates will make expanding grain production for Indonesia progressively more difficult.

Bangladesh has an abundance of water, often too much to maximize crop production. But there is at least the prospect of controlling it. With sufficient investment in water control and irrigation, Bangladesh could boost its grain harvest by four fifths over the next four decades. Because it has water and relatively low yields, it has a greater potential for expanding food production than do many developing countries.

The two countries, both of which now import small amounts of grain, are expected to need substantially greater amounts, even assuming no rise in per capita grain consumption between 1990 and 2030. Although Indonesia is large in population terms, its projected increase during the next four decades is only 62 percent. This helps explain why we estimate its net imports in 2030 at only 12 million tons. The increase in projected imports for Bangladesh to 9 million tons is also relatively modest but largely because of the nation's substantial potential for boosting production.

In Africa, Nigeria and Ethiopia (including Eritrea), are the continent's first and third most populous countries. (Egypt is second.) Both depend heavily on rainfed agriculture, since neither has much irrigation.[6]

Ethiopia faces the addition of 106 million people during the next four decades compared with only 30 million in the last four. Given the difficulty the nation is having providing for the recent addition of 30 million, it is unclear how it could possibly feed another 106 million, particularly since it has some of the world's most severely eroded soils. The reduction in tree cover from 50 percent of the country's land area at the turn of the century to a mere 3 percent today, combined with the steeply sloping nature of much of its cropland, explains the record rates of soil erosion. For Ethiopia, we assume that the increment in grain production in the next four decades will be 4 million tons, double the 2 million tons added in the last 40 years.[7]

Nigeria is in a similar situation in that its projected increase in population by 2030 is 191 million, compared with 55 million since 1950. We assume that it will somehow be able to boost its grain production by 5 million tons during the next four decades, compared with 3 million tons in the last four.

For both these countries, a heavy dependence on semiarid and rainfed agriculture and lack of irrigation potential severely restrict production gains. In Nigeria,

70 percent of the grain harvest consists of millet and sorghum, traditional dryland crops in Africa. It is unlikely that Nigeria can boost yields of these crops by more than half, the gain achieved by Australia's wheat growers since 1950. Given the intensive land degradation and the lack of water for irrigation, both countries are facing challenges on the population front that can be potentially overwhelming.[8]

Ethiopia, even with the optimistic projection of a much greater absolute increase in production during the next four decades than in the last four, still faces an increase in imports to 9 million tons in 2030, and Nigeria an increase to 15 million tons. Filling the deficit projected for Ethiopia alone would take virtually all the grain allocated in the 1994 international food aid program.[9]

In the western hemisphere, the two countries with the largest populations after the United States are Brazil and Mexico, with 150 million and 85 million, respectively. In the next 40 years they are projected to add 99 million and 65 million people, roughly the same as during the last 40. In both countries, the principal food staple is corn, which is supplemented in Mexico by wheat and in Brazil by wheat and rice.[10]

For Mexico, which is facing severe land and water constraints on agricultural growth, we assume production will increase 40 percent. With wheat yields already at a high level, it may be difficult to increase them substantially in the future. With corn, it would be possible to raise output markedly if the traditional, local varieties prized for the quality of their corn meal were replaced with high-yielding hybrids. On the other hand, the rugged mountain terrain on which corn is produced in Mexico has been degraded over the centuries by erosion. In addition, the new arrangements under the General Agreement on Tariffs and Trade will open Mexican agriculture to competition from the outside world, almost certainly reducing its corn output. All in all, a 40-percent expansion in output by 2030 may be the most that can be hoped for.

Projections for Brazil are perhaps the most difficult to make. During the last four decades, Brazil nearly quadrupled its grain harvest, largely by tripling its grain area from 7 million hectares in 1950 to 21 million in 1990. Although grain area has actually contracted somewhat in recent years, we assume that it will expand by perhaps half by 2030, assuming a substantial rise in grain prices. Here we depart from our blanket assumption of no change in prices to illustrate how higher prices can markedly boost production in some cases. This area expansion, combined with a modest further gain in yields, leads us to project an 80-percent increase in output during the next four decades. In its vast cerrado, Brazil has a large area of low fertility land that could be brought under the plow. Unfortunately, this land is marginal and can be profitably farmed only at prices much higher than those currently prevailing.

At current world prices, Brazil is importing all three grains: wheat, rice, and corn. In 1990, it brought in a total of 6 million tons. Since 1950 Brazil boosted its grain harvest by some 27 million tons. During the next four decades, we assume it will raise output by 30 million tons to a total of 67 million tons. Even so, it will still fall somewhat short of the projected demand of 71 million tons in 2030, remaining an importer. Mexico, faced with similar growth in demand but much smaller growth in production, would see its grain import deficit increase from 6 million to 19 million tons.

In sum, during the next 40 years grain consumption in the group of nine more than doubles, climbing to 420 million tons, a reflection of the projected growth in population. Production, meanwhile, continues to lag farther and farther behind consumption. The result is that while consumption doubles, imports more than quadruple, climbing from 32 million tons in 1990 to 147 million tons in 2030.

14

The Growing Imbalance

The individual country projections of grain supply and demand in the last two chapters were more or less "business-as-usual" extrapolations. On the demand side, they assumed that population growth will follow the medium or middle trajectory, that there will be no technological advance leading to a big jump in world food output, and that grain prices will remain stable at the level of the early nineties. On the supply side, they assumed that soil erosion will continue at more or less the recent rate, that the waterlogging and salting of irrigation systems will spread further, that air pollution will keep reducing harvests, that the influx of damaging ultraviolet radiation will continue to rise at least through the end of this decade, and that the concentration of carbon dioxide and other greenhouse gases in the atmosphere will keeping rising.

These projections also take into account the emerging constraints on food output expansion, such as the growing scarcity of fresh water. They recognize that even with gains in water use efficiency, there will be less irrigation in some countries 40 years from now than there is today because of water diversion to nonfarm uses, because pumping has been cut back to balance aquifer recharge, or both. They assume that while new cereal varieties may be marginally more responsive to fertilizer, none will double or triple yields over current high-yielding varieties of wheat, corn, and rice.

To round out the global picture, we review here the production projections for the 13 countries discussed in the last two chapters, and fill in for the rest of the world. For the "big four," the projected net increase in production is 140 million tons. This would be nearly twice as large if China's grain harvest were increasing by one fifth rather than decreasing by that amount. For the other nine nations, all developing ones, the projected increment in output of 106 million tons for the next 40 years is only slightly less than the 110 million tons since 1950. Some countries, such as Bangladesh, will do slightly better in absolute terms; in others, such as Mexico, output will expand less in the next four decades than over the last four.[1]

Combining the projected increases for the two groups yields a total of 246 million tons. If the remaining one third of the world not covered in these projections increases output by roughly the same amount, the world will produce 369 million more tons of grain by the year 2030, for an increase of 9 million tons a year. China greatly affects this calculation: if it were adding 66 million tons of grain to the world output instead of reducing it by that amount, the total during the next four decades would increase by 501 million tons, or more than 12 million tons a year. This is exactly the annual increment that prevailed from 1984 to 1992.[2]

To put this in historical perspective, the annual increase from 1950 to 1984 was 30 million tons. Between 1984 and 1992, it dropped to 12 million tons. And these projections show it dropping further—to 9 million tons between now and 2030.[3]

Looking at the trade implications, the "big four" trade deficit is projected at 204 million tons in 2030, with the lion's share projected for China. Of the group of nine, each was already importing some grain in 1990: five had relatively modest imports of 1–2 million tons, while for Iran, Egypt, Mexico, and Brazil, deficits had already reached 6–8 million tons. But by 2030 all of them except Brazil will be importing vastly larger quantities—for a total deficit of 147 million tons. Brazil, which bought 6 million tons of grain in 1990, is the only one of the nine that is projected to be less dependent on imports.

The total net import deficit for the 13 countries comes to 351 million tons. But one third of the world has not yet been included in the assessment. This includes most of Africa, all of Western Europe, and the smaller countries of Asia and Latin America. For Western Europe, with neither population nor grain consumption per person likely to change much, an exportable surplus of grain is likely to continue even with the recently negotiated reductions in farm price subsidies. Africa, meanwhile, beyond the three populous countries already considered, will be developing a huge deficit. On balance, then, this one third of the world will probably have a net deficit proportionately similar to the other two thirds. If so, the world will be facing import needs that exceed exportable supplies by 526 million tons—an amount approaching the current grain consumption of the United States and China combined.[4]

Other analysts are beginning to sense the potential size of this problem. Peter Hazell, an economist at the International Food Policy Research Institute (IFPRI), projects grain demand in developing countries to 2025, assuming that everyone gets 3,000 calories a day—enough to meet the hidden food needs of the poor. On the supply side, he assumes that the historical rate of rise in yield per hectare will not slow. Even so, his model yields a shortfall in Africa of 215 million tons in 2025. For South Asia, essentially the Indian subcontinent, it yields a deficit of 260 million tons. Thus, for these two regions Hazell projects a net import deficit of 475 million tons in 2025, compared with the 526-million-ton shortfall that we project for 2030 for the entire world.[5]

Hazell sums up the prospect for Africa as particularly scary given the limited potential for dramatically increasing output: "All indicators concur that poverty, malnutrition, and hunger will increase rapidly in Africa in the coming years unless serious action is taken to avoid it." The desperate situation in prospect could lead to deforestation and land degradation on a scale that would threaten the economic and political stability of the region.[6]

Another way of putting the food production prospect in perspective is to look at the availability of the basic inputs—grainland, irrigation water, and fertilizer—under the business-as-usual scenario. For grainland, we assumed that with stable grain prices there would be no appreciable change. From 1990 to 2030, the area in crops would remain at 695 million hectares. There will undoubtedly be net gains in some countries, such as

Brazil, as indicated in Chapter 13. At the same time, in Asia, which will be adding 56 million people per year, cropland losses will be heavy. Rapid industrialization of China and the Indian subcontinent is certain to take a heavy toll.[7]

We also assumed that with constant prices the net irrigated area would expand but quite modestly compared with the historical trend. Future gains will be limited simply because the remaining sites for large-scale irrigation projects are increasingly costly to develop and most cannot be economically justified at current grain prices. It may be unrealistic to expect much gain at all in the net contribution of irrigation to the future growth in output. The inevitable future cutbacks in areas of overpumping to reestablish a balance with aquifer recharge, the diversion of irrigation water to nonfarm uses, and the continuing spread of waterlogging and salting of irrigated land all may combine to offset gains in efficiency and from investment in new irrigation projects.

Fertilizer use is projected to resume growth once the effect of subsidy reductions in key countries wears off. Although it is certain to resume an upward trend, perhaps as early as 1995, it will take many years for fertilizer use even to regain 1989 levels.[8]

The United States is now well into its second decade of no growth in fertilizer use. Barring a marked rise in the genetic yield potential of grain varieties, U.S. fertilizer use is unlikely to expand much in the decades ahead. The same is true for Western Europe and East Asia, including China. Thus in regions that account for half of world food production, there is little reason to expect much growth in fertilizer use.

To get a full picture of the changing food prospect, it is useful to sum up the assumptions regarding both oceanic and land-based food supplies. We expect that the seafood catch in 2030 will be roughly the same as in 1990. (See Table 14–1.) Uniformly good management could raise this somewhat, but equally likely is a continuation of the irresponsible management that is now damaging so many fisheries. This means that the per capita seafood catch would drop from the historical peak of more than 19 kilograms per person in 1990 to 11 kilograms per person in 2030. The effect this will have on seafood prices deserves far more attention than it is getting.[9]

For grain production, the dramatic slowdown under a business-as-usual scenario of constant prices is clear. In contrast to the last 40 years, when it expanded by 1,149 million tons, grain production would increase by only 369 million tons during the next four decades—less than one third as much. If this scenario materializes and if population rises to 8.9 billion, the grain supply per person will drop to 240 kilograms, just 20 percent above the current consumption level of 200 kilograms of India.

Thus far, we have been discussing business-as-usual

TABLE 14-1. *World Seafood Catch and Grain Output, 1950–90, With Projections to 2030*

	1950	1990	2030	Change 1950–90	Projected Change 1990–2030
	(million tons)				
Seafood Catch	22	100	100	+78	0
Grain Output	631	1,780	2,149	+1,149	+369

SOURCE: See endnote 9.

projections. But we do not expect these to materialize, simply because of the widening excess of demand over supply, which shows up in our projections as an excess of import needs over exportable supplies. In the real world, such an imbalance is impossible. Will these projections fail to materialize because production actually expands much faster than we have assumed? Or because population grows slower than projected as governments work to fill the family planning gap and to eliminate the social conditions that foster high fertility? Or because population growth slows as malnutrition raises mortality rates, which is already happening in some African countries?

One unavoidable conclusion is that food prices will rise. The relationship between slower growth in production and food prices is analyzed in an IFPRI projection that assumes that the rise in grain yield per hectare is one fourth lower than the recent historical trend used in an IFPRI baseline projection. By 2010, this results in a rise in wheat prices of 66 percent, in rice prices of 30 percent, and in corn prices of 37 percent. Our scenario, assuming an even slower rise in yields and over a longer time period, will push prices up much more.[10]

After four decades of declining real prices of food, the world may now be on the edge of a period of rising real prices. This has already begun for seafood. As noted in Chapter 5, since 1970 the U.S. index of seafood prices has jumped by one third while those for both beef and poultry have declined.[11]

Rice prices are likely to be the next to rise, simply because this food staple requires not only land but an abundance of water as well. Three consecutive years in which rice consumption exceeded the harvest dropped the carryover stocks in 1994 to the lowest level since

1973, when prices also doubled. When it became clear in September 1993 that Japan would be forced to import up to 2 million tons because of a weather-reduced harvest, the stage was set for a rapid run-up in prices, one that doubled the world rice price within three months.[12]

As of late spring 1994, rice prices have eased as the market has stabilized, dropping part way back to the August 1993 level. Whether they return to the earlier low level will depend on whether the world's rice farmers can rebuild stocks. If rice prices remain high, they will gradually pull wheat prices upward as wheat is substituted for rice. In effect, the world's wheat producers will be satisfying not only the growth in demand for wheat but also some of that for rice.

In a progressively tight supply situation, it is easy to imagine a price rise over time comparable to the doubling of grain prices that occurred between 1972 and 1973. This would help bridge the anticipated excess of demand over supply by simultaneously stimulating greater growth in production than we have projected and checking growth in demand. On the supply side, it would lead to an expansion of cultivation onto land that is now considered economically marginal. The principal concentration of this potential expansion is in Brazil, mostly in the semiarid cerrado region. The net increase in world grain area would not likely be large, simply because the worldwide potential is so limited, but it could conceivably reach 10 percent by 2030.[13]

With irrigation, in some areas water supplies will permit expansion, but it is uneconomical to do so because the cost of large dams and distribution networks is too high relative to grain prices. But even with higher grain prices, the number of sites that can be developed is limited.

In countries that have already passed the agronomic threshold where additional fertilizer increases yields, higher grain prices would have little effect on use. Elsewhere, however, where there is still a substantial unrealized agronomic response that can be exploited, the use of fertilizer could increase substantially.

Higher grain prices would also encourage both public and private investment in agricultural research. Governments would invest more because of their desire to expand food production and check the rise in prices. Seed companies would invest more in varietal improvement because of the higher profit potential.

In analyzing the effect of prices on future food production, it is essential to distinguish between investment areas with limits and those in which higher prices will provide an opportunity for expanding production. If growth in the yield from a fishery comes to a halt because it is being harvested at or beyond its capacity, for example, spending more on fishing boats and nets simply hastens the fishery's collapse. Similarly with irrigation: where water tables are already falling, putting more money into irrigation wells will only hasten depletion of the aquifer and the inevitable reduction in pumping. Higher prices can expand food production by encouraging investment in irrigation projects that are uneconomical under current prices or in the expansion of cropping onto marginal land that cannot be economically farmed at current prices.

If the food situation tightens dramatically and prices begin to climb, it could affect individual childbearing decisions, national population policies, and the family planning efforts of the international community—moving both individual countries and the world as a whole onto a lower population trajectory. As people in more and more countries experience the vulnerability of depending on a volatile food market with unreliable supplies, they may rethink the question of desired family size, leading to smaller families than have been assumed in existing population projections.

At the international level, a tightening food situation could accelerate efforts to fill the family planning gap and to attack the root causes of high fertility. At the national level, countries that face a growing grain deficit may well decide to mobilize quickly to slow population growth in order to avoid spreading hunger or even starvation. Once the dimensions of the emerging food shortages become apparent, it could spur governments to unprecedented levels of activity in creating the conditions that will lower fertility. It is difficult to assess just how quickly things might change, simply because the world will be moving into uncharted territory—into a time when conditions will be far different than any that have prevailed during our lifetimes.

Some sense of how higher prices would reduce grain use can be seen in the United States. After prices doubled between 1972 and 1973, grain use dropped precipitously—from 148 million tons in 1972 to 101 million tons in 1974. This decrease, all of it in the use of grain as feed, would cover 10 percent of the 526-million-ton shortfall we project for 2030. But this reduction was price-related and therefore temporary. As the seventies progressed and prices eased, feedgrain use resumed its historical rise.[14]

Another possibility for lightening the demands on world grain supplies is a reduction in per capita grain use in affluent societies for health reasons. As people become more health-conscious and aware of the detrimental effect of excessive consumption of fat-rich livestock products, they may reduce consumption. There is a precedent for a major life-style change for health reasons in the United States in the dramatic decline in cigarette smoking.[15]

Yet the higher grain prices that reduce consumption of livestock products in affluent societies can be life-threatening to those in low-income countries. For the millions who are already spending 70 percent or more of their income on food, a doubling of grain prices can threaten survival. The groups most directly affected are the rural landless and the low-income urban residents.[16]

If governments decide they want to reduce grain consumption, either to increase exports or to reduce imports, they have two well-defined policy tools that can be used for this purpose. One is to ration consumption of the livestock products that require large amounts of grain. Many governments have used food rationing before, including the United States and several European countries during World War II.

The second tool is a tax on the consumption of livestock products in order to reduce feed use of grain, freeing more for direct human consumption. Again, this can be used by both exporting and importing countries. In addition to its beneficial health effect in affluent societies, it could also incorporate some of the indirect environmental costs of producing livestock: overgrazing, irrigation overpumping, and pollution from feedlots. Of the two approaches, taxes are easier to administer, but rationing can be more equitable.

One way to increase the supply of grain for food is to reduce nonfood uses. In the United States, for example, in 1993 some 10 million tons of corn were used to produce roughly 1 billion gallons of ethanol as an additive to gasoline to help it burn more cleanly and to reduce pollution. But there are other compounds that can be used for this purpose that are not derived from food-stuffs. Diverting this 10 million tons of corn from fuel production to food or feed uses would cut the projected shortfall of 526 million tons by 2 percent.[17]

Another area of potential gain lies in the reduction of post-harvest losses, which are greatest in developing countries where grain is stored locally. Much grain is damaged by rain or lost to insects in storage. It is relatively easy to upgrade storage facilities in large grain elevators around cities and ports, but far more difficult to do so when it involves millions of tiny storage facilities, as it does in a country such as India, where nearly 60 million farmers store their annual household grain supply. Nonetheless, if grain prices rise, investing in storage improvements will become far more profitable and could save substantial quantities of grain.[18]

Aside from reducing consumption of livestock products, there is a broad potential for improving the efficiency of feedgrain use. Within developing countries, in particular, the efficiency with which grain is converted into beef, pork, poultry, or milk can be greatly improved, which collectively could save millions of tons of grain. Beyond this, farmers could shift to the more efficient forms of meat—from beef to poultry, for example, or pork to poultry. This is actually already occurring, since beef production has not increased at all in recent years while poultry production continues its rapid growth. If recent trends continue, we project that poultry production will overtake beef by the end of this decade.[19]

On the other side of the equation is the growing pressure on croplands from the levelling off of the world fish catch and of the production of livestock products from rangelands. Until recently, growth in the seafood catch provided 2 million additional tons of protein-rich food each year and growth in rangeland production yielded another million tons of beef and mutton. In theory, this gap could be filled by farming fish and putting cattle in feedlots, but expanding aquacultural output by 2 million tons annually would take 4 million tons of additional grain per year. By 2030, this would total 160 million tons, roughly the amount that India now consumes. For beef, an additional million tons per year would take 7 million tons of grain, or 280 million tons per year by 2030.[20]

To answer the question "How many people can the earth support?" it is important to ask "At what level of consumption?" Whether or not we have a full house depends on where we want to live on the food chain. If we would like to continue to consume as much seafood as we do now, then the house is clearly full, because the future promises progressively less seafood with each passing year. If those living in developing countries want to consume more livestock products, moving up to the levels of industrial societies, then again the house is clearly full, because the grain supply needed to support this diet diversification is simply not in prospect.

Many of the world's people aspire to the U.S. diet, which requires some 800 kilograms of grain per person a year. Others would be quite happy with much less. But few would volunteer to live on the average grain consumption in India today—200 kilograms a year. In a business-as-usual world, one that will be adding 3.6 billion people during the next four decades, the only real question is whether the average global grain consumption per person in 2030 will be closer to China's current 300 kilograms a year or to India's. Although there are numerous ways of cutting the less essential uses of grain, including those just discussed, it is difficult to see how an acceptable balance between food and people can be achieved without a broad-based reduction in population growth.[21]

V

Taking
Charge

15

Reassessing Population Policy

With fishers and farmers no longer able to expand output fast enough to keep up with population growth, it is time to reassess population policy. New information on the carrying capacity of both land and oceanic food systems argues for a basic rethinking of national population policies, an accelerated international response to fill unmet family planning needs, and a recasting of development strategies to address the underlying causes of high fertility.

As national demands cross the sustainable-yield thresholds of local fisheries, rangelands, and aquifers, the resource base itself is being consumed. In some situations, the question may not be what rate of population growth is sustainable but whether growth can continue without reducing living standards and jeopardizing the prospect of future generations.

The seafood catch is unlikely to expand beyond the recent level of 100 million tons, so the seafood supply per person will decline for as long as population grows. A decade hence, the same amount of fish that is caught today will be shared among an additional 900 million people; prices will be far higher and on average each of us will eat much less seafood. Similarly, it is now difficult to see how farmers can keep up with population growth as projected. The bottom line is that achieving a humane balance between people and food supplies may now depend far more on family planners than on fishers and farmers.[1]

The world grain harvest of 2.1 billion tons in 2030 could satisfy populations of different sizes, depending on consumption levels. At the U.S. consumption level of 800 kilograms per person per year, it would sustain roughly 2.5 billion people. At the Italian consumption level of 400 kilograms, it could support just over 5 billion, roughly the 1990 world population. And at the Indian level of 200 kilograms, a harvest of 2.1 billion tons would support just over 10 billion people. Although many people aspire to the U.S. diet, population growth has foreclosed that option for much of humanity for the foreseeable future.[2]

At its peak of 346 kilograms in 1984, world grain output per person was well above the current average of roughly 300 kilograms of China and climbing toward the 400 kilograms of Italy. But that trend has been reversed. In 1993, the average was down to 303 kilograms. The projected harvest in 2030 would provide 240 kilograms for each of the 8.9 billion people projected for that year—some 29 percent below the 1984 historical high. Stated otherwise, average grain consumption per person for 2030 would be well below that of China today and would be approaching that of India.[3]

Coming at a time when U.N. estimates show 900 million people in developing countries already failing to get enough calories to maintain normal levels of physical activity and when 36 percent of preschool children in developing countries are below weight for their age, this projected decline is not a pleasant prospect.[4]

In a world where per capita supplies of both seafood and grain are falling, the need for rethinking population policy is obvious. Even now, the food needs of the 90 million added each year can be satisfied only by reducing consumption among those already here.

Concern about the effects of continuing rapid population growth has spread beyond the population, development, and environmental communities to much of the scientific community. During the last two years or so, the international scientific community has issued several warnings of the potential dangers that lie ahead if rapid population growth continues.

As mentioned in Chapter 1, in November 1993 an international conference of representatives of national science academies gathered in New Delhi at their first ever summit conference. They considered the population threat in its many dimensions, and were concerned about the effect of continuing population growth on human welfare. The delegates concluded that the only sensible population policy for the world was population stabilization, and argued that this should be achieved during the lifetimes of their children, which would be around 2040.[5]

The statement issued at the end of the conference, which was endorsed by some 56 science academies, urged governments to adopt an "integrated policy on population and sustainable development." It pointed out that reducing fertility rates was not simply a matter of providing more contraceptives, but that family planning had to be part of broader reproductive health services for women, along with efforts to meet other basic needs, such as the provision of clean water.[6]

In April 1994, the United Nations Population Fund, the U.N. agency responsible for population and family planning, put forth a proposal to stabilize world population at 7.8 billion by the year 2050. Among other things, the plan calls for quadrupling funding for international family planning assistance programs, pushing the total to $4.4 billion by 2000. The program is broad-based, involving changes in the role of women and the expansion of family planning services to include both the 120 million couples who want to use family planning services but cannot get them and an additional 230 million couples who would need to plan their families if population is to stabilize at the 7.8 billion level.[7]

The Population Fund plan calls for providing universal primary education for both girls and boys and making secondary education available to at least half of all girls. It is also designed to reduce infant mortality in developing countries from 69 deaths for every 1,000 births to 12, the current rate in the industrial world. If implemented, this program would move the world onto a low-growth path where population would rise from today's 5.5 billion to 7.27 billion in 2015 and stabilize at 7.8 billion in 2050.[8]

Given the limits to the carrying capacity of each country's land and water resources, every national government now needs a carefully articulated and adequately supported population policy, one that takes into account the country's carrying capacity at whatever consumption level citizens decide on. As Harvard biologist Edward O. Wilson observes in his landmark book *The Diversity of Life*, "Every nation has an economic policy and a foreign policy. The time has come to speak more openly of a population policy. By this I mean not just the capping of growth when the population hits the wall, as in China and India, but a policy based on a rational solution of this problem; what, in the judgment of its informed citizenry, is the *optimal* population?"[9]

In addition to recognizing the basic right to control fertility and the benefits of family planning to health and well-being, governments need to integrate food carrying capacity into population policy. Few national political leaders even use the term carrying capacity, much less incorporate the concept into policymaking. The potential social costs of carrying capacity overruns discussed in earlier chapters should inform policymaking and could help mobilize public support for improving access to high-quality reproductive health and family planning services and for encouraging smaller families.

As a starting point, governments can calculate their population carrying capacity by estimating the land available for crops, the amount of water that will be available for irrigation over the long term, and the yield of crops based on what the most advanced countries with similar growing conditions have achieved. Without such a calculation, governments are simply flying blind into the future, drifting into a world in which population growth and environmental degradation lead to social disintegration. Once projections of future food supplies are completed, then societies can consider what policies relating to population size and consumption levels are appropriate.[10]

Governments of countries where the carrying capacity

assessments show growing grain deficits may assume
they can cover these with imports. But the projected
growth in national grain deficits collectively dwarfs that
of grain surpluses. Indeed, the world's leading grain exporter, the United States, has actually experienced a decline in its exportable surplus in the last decade.[11]

Closely associated with the calculations of population
carrying capacity at various levels of consumption is the
need for a public education effort to acquaint people
with all the benefits of family planning and small families. Simply filling the family planning gap would reduce
markedly the average family size in many developing
countries. Beyond this, population experts believe that
improved family planning services together with educational and health programs focused on women can eventually stabilize population through delays in childbearing and choices for small families.[12]

People need to know the long-term consequences of
having an average of, say, six children, four children, or
two children. Couples who have this information may
realize that the key question is no longer "How many
children should I have for my old age security?" but
"How will the number of children I have affect their
lives and the world in which they will live?" Since people
everywhere care deeply about their children, answering
this question can help spawn an important shift in thinking, one with a potentially profound effect on family size
decisions. If population policy does not include public
discussion of these options, it is less likely to succeed.

Some 25 countries, with 700 million people, have essentially stabilized their population size. This group,
home to one eighth of the world's population, has done
what many other countries may decide they also must
do as they analyze their population carrying capacity.[13]

As the gravity of the food situation begins to unfold, what may be emerging is a greater emphasis on reproductive responsibilities relative to traditional reproductive rights in terms of couples being able to have as many children as they wanted. In addition to individual couples asking whether they can afford more than two children, an increasingly relevant question may be whether local fisheries, rangelands, and croplands can support more than two children per couple. In June 1994, even the Pontifical Academy of Sciences, a lay panel at the Vatican, released a study on population that recognized it is "unthinkable to sustain indefinitely a birth rate that notably exceeds the level of two children per couple." At issue is how to balance the reproductive rights of the current generation with the survival rights of the next generation.[14]

Many societies may realize that they are in a new situation, one in which they need to stabilize population size quickly. In countries that now have stable populations, this process was spread over many decades, if not a century or two. Societies facing food scarcity may realize the importance of slowing population growth quickly by shifting to smaller families before nature assumes the responsibility for doing so. This will take many governments into new territory.

The obvious first step is to fill the family planning gap, to make certain that the 120 million or more women who already want to limit the size of their families but are unable to do so are given access to family planning services. The Rockefeller Foundation has made this the principal goal of its population program.[15]

At present, the total fertility rate for the world is roughly four children per couple. In a set of conservative calculations, Steve Sinding of the Rockefeller Foundation estimates that filling the family planning gap would reduce this to three, thus cutting in half the gap between current fertility and replacement-level fertility.[16]

In February 1994, Department of State Counselor Tim Wirth announced that the United States was committed to making sure that by the end of this decade no woman who wanted family planning services was denied access to them. The U.S. government has committed itself to increasing funding from $585 million in 1994 to $1.2 billion in the year 2000. This is a major step forward and an example of the importance of U.S. leadership. It is likely that Japan and other governments will lend their support to this goal.[17]

Even as the family planning gap is being filled, there is a need to deal with the underlying social causes of high fertility. Improved literacy plays an important role, for example, not only because among females it correlates closely with reducing fertility, but also because for farmers it is often the key to the adoption of more sophisticated agricultural management practices. At a time when some planners are already worrying about computer literacy in the Third World, hundreds of millions of people still lack the rudimentary skills to take advantage of Gutenberg's printing press, invented some five centuries ago.[18]

A United Nations–led effort to achieve universal literacy, patterned after its highly successful effort to promote childhood immunizations, could appeal to the ideals and energy of young people throughout the world. Equally urgent is the need to improve the status of women, particularly in developing countries, where females suffer discrimination from birth. In addition, any strategy that reduces poverty sets the stage for a shift to small families.[19]

Apart from what individual countries decide about their population/resource balances, we now know from the global data that the world is facing a difficult situation. It is time for world leaders—the heads of international institutions and national governments—to speak out.

If the world were to collectively address the population issue on a scale commensurate with the human suffering that is almost inevitable if rapid population growth continues, population-related issues would be addressed regularly at national cabinet meetings and at sessions of the U.N. General Assembly. World leaders would ensure universal access to family planning and reproductive health care, and would urge people to have small families. In discussions among political leaders, changes in birth rates would get at least as much attention as changes in employment or interest rates. Gains in female literacy would rank in importance with gains in savings rates.

Unabated rapid population growth, which once slowed the rise in living standards, is now lowering them for large segments of humanity. Unfortunately, there is as yet little recognition in political discourse that the nature of the population threat has changed dramatically in recent years—that the population growth that once slowed progress is now reversing it for much of humanity.

16

Turning the Tide

The four-decade span from 1950 to 1990 was a period of remarkable worldwide progress, one with gains on a scale that had no precedent. During this period, incomes were rising, living conditions were improving, and life expectancy climbed from 46 to 64 years.[1]

Underpinning this progress was an unprecedented increase in world food production, boosting grain consumption per person some 40 percent and more than doubling seafood consumption per person. Now these trends have been reversed. With every passing year, we can each expect to have less seafood to eat. With every passing year, the amount of grain we each can consume directly or as livestock products—meat, milk, cheese, eggs, and yogurt—will be diminishing.[2]

After nearly four decades of unprecedented progress,

it is hard for us to imagine how different conditions will be in the decades ahead if we continue with business as usual. The 90 million people being added each year can be fed only if consumption is reduced among those already here. At the national level, more and more governments will have to choose between more people and better diets, putting population policy in a new light.[3]

The food sector is the first where our demands are colliding with some of the earth's limits—the capacity of oceanic fisheries to supply fish, of the hydrological cycle to supply fresh water, and of crop varieties to respond to fertilizer. The impact of these collisions will reverberate throughout the economy in ways we cannot now even imagine. In these circumstances, the need to address directly the carrying capacity question—How many people can the earth support and at what level of consumption?—is obvious.

These new trends in seafood catch and grain production promise a future not just of spreading hunger in Africa, but of global food scarcity, a future where the real price of food, declining since mid-century, will probably rise. This is already evident with seafood, with prices ratcheting upward. Given the land and water constraints on the production of rice, the staple food for much of humanity, its price could also soon start a long-term climb. If that happens, the price of wheat can be expected to follow.

Of all economic indicators, none is more politically sensitive than food prices. If supplies tighten, as the carrying capacity assessments in Chapters 12 and 13 suggest, rising prices could present a difficult challenge to governments everywhere. As the politics of surplus is replaced by a politics of scarcity, higher food prices and inflation threats in exporting countries could lead to grain export restrictions or even outright embargoes, as happened in the mid-seventies after grain prices doubled.[4]

Although the international community can provide leadership and offer guidance, it is national governments that will decide the fate of people. They allocate most of the resources, formulate population and agricultural policies, and decide how resources are distributed. International food assistance will be available, but even if it were several times its current scale, it would be trivial compared with needs. In the end, only national governments can assume the responsibility for feeding their people.

As the food/population balance becomes more precarious, concern about potential climate instability will escalate in parallel with the rise in atmospheric concentrations of greenhouse gases. In a time of food scarcity, climate disruption becomes an even greater threat. Dealing with the effects of global warming while trying to cope with scarcity will put great stress on governments.

As noted earlier, Robert Kaplan has written eloquently about rapid population growth and environmental degradation leading to social disintegration, political fragmentation, and the spread of anarchy. If we add to these forces food scarcity and the political stresses associated with rising food prices, it is easy to visualize the disintegration of weaker nation-states and the emergence of a population-driven environmental deterioration/economic decline scenario.[5]

Many countries, a majority of them in Africa, are now moving along such a path. If this continues, deteriorating ecosystems and food scarcity will generate massive flows of environmental refugees, movements that will themselves lead to territorial conflicts and overwhelm national borders. Because this is an out-of-control situation, it is difficult to visualize the form it will take.

Against this backdrop, the drop in grain output per person is not merely an agronomic trend: it is an indicator of the increasingly troubled relationship between us, now 5.5 billion in number, and the natural systems and resources on which we depend. We are now beginning to get some glimpses of how this deteriorating relationship affects our social systems. It is a systemic threat that requires a systemic response. At the most fundamental level, we need to recognize that we are approaching a potential crisis and that we need to respond on an appropriate scale.[6]

As we enter uncharted territory, we now need a new vision to guide us, a sense of where we want to go. If we want a stable, peaceful future, we have no choice but to actively intervene and reverse the deterioration/decline scenario. If we do not, and instead continue with business as usual, then the Kaplan scenario will materialize in more and more areas.

Future food security cannot be separated from environmental sustainability. The challenge is to build an economic system that is environmentally sustainable. The threats to this—population growth, deforestation, soil erosion, aquifer depletion, air pollution, greenhouse gas emissions, and the decimation of plant and animal species—are the same forces that threaten future food security.

Elements of a global food and population strategy are beginning to emerge. In April 1994, the United Nations Population Fund (UNFPA, from its original name) sketched the outlines of a bold effort to stabilize world population at 7.8 billion by the year 2050. This plan is a broad-based one that includes filling the family planning gap, raising the level of female education, and pressing for equal rights for women in all societies. There is no reasonable alternative to such an effort.[7]

UNFPA has presented a budget for the family planning part of this program. As noted in Chapter 15, it includes providing counselling and services not only to the 120 million women who want to limit the size of their families but who lack the means to do so, but also to an additional 230 million couples who will need to plan their families if population is to stabilize by 2050.

In the early years, the budget also provides for the training of family planning workers, which is one of the keys to the rapid expansion of services. But the program does more than just provide family planning services. It includes information activities for public education, such as working with the mass media and schools, and the expansion of reproductive health care. It also has a component to control sexually transmitted diseases, including, importantly, the spread of the HIV virus. And finally, it covers the population data collection, analysis, and dissemination needed for public education and policy formulation.

Implementing the proposed UNFPA Programme of Action requires an estimated $11.4 billion in 1996, gradually rising to $14.4 billion in 2005. (See Table 16–1.) Of this total, roughly two thirds is to be mobilized within developing countries themselves. The complementary resource flows from donor countries would increase to $4.4 billion (1993 dollars) in 2000, rising further to $4.8 billion in 2005.[8]

Achieving the UNFPA's fertility reduction goals requires substantial increases in female education. Although this contributes simultaneously to economic

TABLE 16-1. *Global Food Security Budget*

Year	Family Planning	Primary Education	Adult Literacy	Refores- tation	Soil Conser- vation	Agric. & Forest Research	Total
			(billion dollars)				
1996	11.4	3.0	2.0	2.4	4.5	1.0	24.3
1997	11.8	4.0	2.5	3.2	9.1	2.0	32.6
1998	12.3	5.0	3.0	4.4	13.6	3.0	41.3
1999	12.7	6.0	3.5	5.2	18.1	4.0	49.5
2000	13.2	6.5	4.0	5.6	24.0	5.0	58.3
2001	13.4	6.6	4.0	6.0	24.0	5.0	59.0
2002	13.7	6.7	4.0	6.4	24.0	5.0	59.8
2003	13.9	6.8	4.0	6.4	24.0	5.0	60.1
2004	14.2	6.9	4.0	6.8	24.0	5.0	60.9
2005	14.4	7.0	4.0	6.8	24.0	5.0	61.2

SOURCE: See endnote 8.

progress and lower fertility, in many countries, such as Nepal, Ethiopia, and Senegal, fewer than half the girls of primary-school age are in class. Almost all governments have adopted universal primary education as a goal, but many have seen their educational system overwhelmed by the sheer number of children entering school. The governments of high-fertility societies cannot realistically hope to rein in population growth without broadening access to education and thus providing women with options beyond childbearing.[9]

Fulfilling this social condition for a more rapid fertility decline will require a heavy investment in both school building and teacher training. Providing elementary education for the estimated 130 million school-age children not now in school (70 percent of whom are female) would cost roughly $6.5 billion per year. Providing literacy training for those men and women who are illiterate and beyond school age would require an additional estimated $4 billion per year.[10]

On the food side of the equation, we have focused in Table 16–1 on protecting the soil and water resource base and increasing the investment in agricultural research. At the root of food scarcity in many developing countries is the loss of vegetation from deforestation, overgrazing, and overplowing. As vegetation is destroyed, rainfall runoff increases, reducing aquifer recharge, increasing soil erosion, and, in turn, lowering the inherent productivity of the ecosystem.

Where firewood is scarce, crop residues are burned for cooking fuel, thus depriving the soil of needed organic matter. Adding trees to the global forest stock is a valuable investment in our economic future, whether the goal is to satisfy the growing firewood needs in the Third World or to stabilize soil and water regimes. Accordingly, we have included in our global food security budget a massive reforestation plan—totalling $5.6 billion a year early by the end of the decade.[11]

More than a billion people live in countries that are already experiencing firewood shortages. Unless corrective action is taken, that number will nearly double by the year 2000. An estimated 55 million hectares of tree planting will be needed to meet the fuelwood demand expected then. In addition, anchoring soils and restoring hydrological stability in thousands of Third World watersheds will require tree planting on some 100 million hectares.[12]

Considering that some trees would serve both fuelwood and ecological objectives, a total of 120 million hectares might need to be planted. An additional 30 million hectares will be needed to satisfy demand for lumber, both local and for export, and for paper manufacturing. If this tree planting goal is to be achieved during the next decade, the effort would need to proceed somewhat along the lines outlined in Table 16–1, with annual plantings gradually expanding during the next several years.

Estimating the cost of reforesting an area equivalent to 150 million hectares varies widely, according to the approach taken. Numerous studies by the World Bank and other development agencies show costs ranging from $200 to $500 per hectare for trees planted by farmers as part of agroforestry activities, and up to $2,000 or more for commercial plantations. Farmers' costs are lower mainly because the labor to plant, maintain, and protect the trees is contributed by the family. The effort is seen as an investment in family welfare, much as home gardening uses family labor to reduce food expenditures.[13]

In estimating the cost of establishing tree cover, it is assumed that the great bulk of the 150 million hectares will be planted by local villagers and that the average cost will be $400 per hectare including seedling costs. At this rate, tree planting expenditures would total some $53 billion, just under $6 billion per year during the next decade.[14]

Planting trees to restore watersheds, thereby conserving soil and water, complements the expenditures on soil conservation by farmers. To calculate the cost of a global effort to stabilize soils, data are used from the United States, where it is estimated that roughly $3 billion a year would be needed to stabilize soils on U.S. cropland.[15]

First, it is assumed that one tenth of the world's cropland cannot sustain cultivation with any economically

feasible soil-conserving agricultural practices—roughly
the same proportion as in the United States. This would
equal some 128 million hectares worldwide. Applying
the cost of converting such land to grassland or woodland in the United States, at $125 per hectare as a first
approximation, the global cost would be $16 billion per
year. If expenditures to conserve topsoil on the remaining erosion-prone cropland, another 100 million hectares, are comparable to these (disregarding, for the purpose of illustration, the vast differences in land tenure
and farming methods that characterize farming in different regions), a global program of conservation practices
enacted by 2000 would cost an additional $8 billion an-
nually.[16]

By 2000, when both the cropland conversion program
and the full range of needed soil-conserving practices
are in place, global expenditures to protect the cropland
base would total some $24 billion per year. Although
this is obviously a large sum, it is less than the U.S.
government has paid farmers to support crop prices in
some years. As a down payment on future food supplies
for a world expecting at least 2 billion more people, $24
billion is an investment humanity can ill afford not to
make.[17]

At a time when the backlog of yield-raising technologies is shrinking, international expenditures on agricultural research are diminishing. The urgency of reversing
this trend is obvious. A remarkably successful international network of 17 agricultural research institutes,
ranging from the International Maize and Wheat Improvement Center in Mexico to the International Rice
Research Institute in the Philippines, identifies gaps in
global agricultural research and systematically fills
them. Tied together under the Washington-based Con-

sultative Group on International Agricultural Research, this network is the source of many agricultural advances of the last few decades.

As noted in Chapter 10, despite its widely recognized success, funding of this network, which climbed from $20 million in 1972 to $319 million in 1992, has dropped to an estimated $285 million in 1994—a decline of more than one tenth. We are proposing that investment in the international network of 17 research institutes be increased to $500 million by 2000. At a time when every technological advance, however small, is needed to help buy time to slow population growth, investment in these centers should be rising, not falling.[18]

Beyond the funding of this key network, there is a need to expand agricultural and forestry research broadly in the effort to boost food production on a sustainable basis. Among the more pressing research needs are deforestation, soil conservation, and the adaptation of internationally available technologies to local conditions. The World Bank estimates that filling this gap would take $5 billion per year.[19]

In summary, the food security budget outlined here, including needed expenditures on both sides of the food/population equation, would start at $24 billion in 1996, increasing rapidly to just over $58 billion in the year 2000 and then grow much more slowly, reaching $61 billion by 2005. At the 2005 level, this would amount to less than one fourth of current U.S. military expenditures. Although the budget is described as a food security budget, it is also a political stability budget—an investment in an environmentally sustainable, politically stable future.[20]

The growth in food output is also being slowed by the

decline in public investment in agriculture in developing countries, particularly in building the physical infrastructure needed to support agricultural progress. This includes farm-to-market roads, improved local grain storage facilities, and irrigation system maintenance. At the institutional level, there is a need for an extension service not only to disseminate new technologies from the research stations, but also to help farmers adopt soil-conserving farming practices and increase irrigation efficiency.

Aside from the global food security budget, which involves public expenditures, there are several needs that are best satisfied by reforming economic policies, specifically those that deal with water efficiency and global warming. With water becoming increasingly scarce, future gains in irrigation depend heavily on the more efficient use of irrigation water. The key to this is to remove the subsidies that provide farmers with free water or water at a nominal cost. Only if farmers pay market costs for water will they make the needed investments in irrigation efficiency.[21]

In a related area, much progress has been made in recent years in reducing fertilizer subsidies, a practice that often led to excessive fertilizer use and damaging levels of nutrient runoff into rivers and lakes. Subsidy reduction or elimination in major food-producing countries, such as the former Soviet Union, India, and China, has helped eliminate excessive fertilizer use.[22]

The other area needing major reform is the tax system, which should be restructured so that those who burn fossil fuels pay the full costs of their use. As it now stands, a utility company that burns coal pays only for the costs associated with extracting and burning it, while others are left to bear the indirect costs of air pollution—

health care costs, crop losses, and the damage from acid rain to forests and freshwater lakes. The motorist driving down the road never pays for the crop damage in the adjoining fields caused by pollution from the automobile.

Similarly, those who burn fossil fuels are not paying the costs of global warming and overall climate instability. An estimated $200 billion is required just to deal with adjustments in the irrigation system associated with global warming. Insurance companies are already raising premiums on housing insurance in some regions, such as the southeastern United States, to cover increased damage from greater storm intensity. Accordingly, we recommend a restructuring of the tax system to partially replace income taxes with taxes on fossil fuels. This would help offset the inability of the market to fully incorporate costs, steering the evolution of the global energy economy in an environmentally sustainable direction.[23]

There is a dangerous perception today that the world is adrift, with no clear sense of where to go and how to get there. The loss of hope associated with this situation, particularly among those already caught in the deterioration/decline scenario, is dangerous and can be destructive. The investments we have outlined in family planning, tree planting, and literacy can help restore hope, giving people a sense that the future can be better.

The need now is for world leaders to seize the initiative, for a bold new effort similar to the Marshall Plan launched in 1947. When the United States announced this plan to rebuild war-torn economies, including adversary and ally alike, it changed the way governments think about war and particularly its aftermath. The traditional "pillage and plunder" approach had been replaced by "rebuild and restore." It redefined the behavior expected of countries after a war, setting the stage for an era of unprecedented international cooperation.

Only the United Nations can manage an effort to reverse the environmental degradation of the planet. The UN has distinguished itself with the boldness of its initiatives on several occasions. For example, the World Health Organization led the highly successful effort to eradicate smallpox, literally banishing this age-old plague from the face of the earth. A decade ago, UNICEF launched a highly successful worldwide program to immunize all the world's children. And most recently, as noted, UNFPA has outlined a comprehensive strategy to stabilize population by 2050.[24]

Even as these steps are being taken, there is a need for a detailed assessment of the earth's population carrying capacity. Such a study could be done by the United Nations or by a member government. Once completed, this study could be used to refine both international and national strategies. Without such an assessment, it is very difficult for national governments to have a clear sense of what, for example, the world's food market will look like in the decades ahead.

It cannot be argued that resources are not available to reverse the deteriorating relationship between ourselves and the natural systems and resources on which we depend. Despite the end of the cold war, the world is still spending close to $700 billion for military purposes, much of it designed to deal with threats that have long since disappeared.[25]

If national security is defined to address the threats facing the world in the mid-nineties, it will lead to a massive redirection of resources. To cite just one specific example, the U.S. government spends $30 billion a year on military intelligence. UNFPA, the lead agency in the effort to stabilize world population, has an annual budget of $240 million. If continuing population growth is the threat to political stability that we believe it is, then having a U.N. Population Fund budget that is less than 1 percent of the U.S. military intelligence budget is indefensible.[26]

Seldom has the world faced an unfolding emergency whose dimensions are as clear as the growing imbalance between food and people. The new information on the earth's carrying capacity brings with it a responsibility to educate and to act that, until recently, did not exist. A massive global environmental education effort, one in which the communications media is heavily involved, may be the only way to bring about the needed transformation in the time available.

If the world is to move off the path of potential deterioration and decline onto one that is environmentally sustainable, there is a need for leadership. The United Nations can and should play the lead role. But if the United States does not step forward and strongly support it, it is unlikely that the United Nations will be able to do it, particularly given the preoccupation of the Secretary General with day-to-day peacekeeping crises.

The measure of individuals or nations is whether they respond to the great issues of their time. For our generation, the challenge is to reverse the deteriorating food situation, achieving a balance between people and food that is both humane and sustainable. And this, in turn, depends on reversing the deteriorating relationship between ourselves, currently increasing by 90 million per year, and the natural systems and resources on which we depend.

Notes

CHAPTER 1. Entering a New Era

1. U.S. Department of Agriculture (USDA), Economic Research Service (ERS), "World Grain Database" (unpublished printout), Washington, D.C., 1992; U.N. Food and Agriculture Organization (FAO), *Yearbook of Fishery Statistics: Catches and Landings* (Rome: various years), with updates for 1991 and 1992 data from FAO, Rome, private communication, April 29, 1993.
2. Table 1-1 is from USDA, op. cit. note 1, and from FAO, op. cit. note 1; FAO, *FAO Production Yearbooks* (Rome: varoius years).
3. FAO, op. cit. note 1; World Resources Institute, *World Resources 1990-91* (New York: Oxford University Press, 1991).
4. FAO, *1948-1985 World Crop and Livestock Statistics* (Rome: 1987); FAO, *FAO Production Yearbooks* (Rome: 1988 through 1991); USDA, "World Agricultural Production," Washington, D.C., August 1992 and March 1993; Worldwatch estimates.
5. "Justus von Liebig" and "Gregor Mendel," *Encyclopaedia Britannica* (Cambridge, Mass.: Encyclopaedia Britannica, Inc., 1976); "History of Agriculture," ibid.; Joseph A. Tainter, *The Collapse of*

Complex Societies (New York: Cambridge University Press, 1988).

6. G. Thottappilly et al., eds., *Biotechnology: Enhancing Research on Tropical Crops in Africa* (Ibadan, Nigeria: International Institute of Tropical Agriculture and Technical Centre for Agricultural and Rural Cooperation, 1992).

7. USDA, op. cit. note 1.

8. Donald N. Duvick, "Intensification of Known Technology and Prospects of Breakthroughs in Technology and Future Food Supply," Iowa State University, Johnston, Iowa, February 1994.

9. Mark Trumbull, "Pacific Northwest Fisheries Shrink, Taking Thousands of Jobs Away," *Christian Science Monitor*, March 28, 1994; Victoria Griffith, "Too Few Fish in the Sea," *Financial Times*, May 27, 1992; FAO, *Fishery Statistics: Catches and Landings* (Rome: 1993).

10. Gordon Sloggett and Clifford Dickason, *Ground-Water Mining in the United States* (Washington, D.C.: USDA, ERS, 1986); Sandra Postel, *Last Oasis: Facing Water Scarcity* (New York: W.W. Norton & Company, 1992).

11. FAO, *Fertilizer Yearbook* (Rome: 1991); International Fertilizer Industry Association (IFA), *Fertilizer Consumption Report* (Paris: 1992).

12. USDA, ERS, "Production, Supply, and Demand View" (electronic database), Washington, D.C., November 1993.

13. Ibid.

14. Robert Kaplan, "The Coming Anarchy," *Atlantic Monthly*, February 1994.

15. Ibid.

16. Royal Society of London and the U.S. National Academy of Sciences, *Population Growth, Resource Consumption, and a Sustainable World* (London and Washington, D.C.: 1992).

17. Union of Concerned Scientists, "World's Leading Scientists Issue Urgent Warning to Humanity," Washington, D.C., press release, November 18, 1992.

18. K. S. Jayaraman, "Science Academies Call for Global Goal of Zero Population Growth," *Nature*, November 4, 1993.

19. U.S. Bureau of the Census data, published in Francis Urban and Ray Nightingale, *World Population by Country and Region, 1950–90 and Projections to 2050* (Washington, D.C.: USDA, ERS, 1993).

20. Ibid.; production data from USDA, op. cit. note 1; Donald O. Mitchell and Merlinda D. Ingco, International Economics Department, *The World Food Outlook* (Washington, D.C.: World Bank, 1993); Nikos Alexandratos, "The Outlook for World

Food and Agriculture to the Year 2010," FAO, Rome, February 1994.

CHAPTER 2. Food Insecurity

1. United Nations Development Programme (UNDP), *Human Development Report 1993* (New York: Oxford University Press, 1993).
2. U.S. Department of Agriculture (USDA), Economic Research Service (ERS), "Production, Supply, and Demand Views" (electronic database), Washington, D.C., November 1993; 1950–59 data from USDA, ERS, "World Grain Database" (unpublished printout), Washington, D.C., 1992.
3. Figure 2–1 is from USDA, "Production, Supply, and Demand Views," op. cit. note 2, from USDA, "World Grain Database," op. cit. note 2, and from U.S. Bureau of the Census, "Midyear Population and Average Annual Growth Rates for the World: 1950–1995" (unpublished printout), Suitland, Md., March 25, 1993.
4. USDA, "Production, Supply, and Demand View," op. cit. note 2; USDA, "World Grain Database," op. cit. note 2.
5. USDA, "World Grain Database," op. cit. note 2.
6. Figure 2–2 is from USDA, "Production, Supply, and Demand View," op. cit. note 2, and from USDA, "World Grain Database," op. cit. note 2.
7. Rice prices from Chicago Trade Board, private communication, November 5, 1993; 1994 stock numbers from USDA, "Production, Supply, and Demand View," op. cit. note 2.
8. USDA, ERS, *Agricultural Resources: Cropland, Water and Conservation Situation and Outlook Report*, Washington, D.C., September 1991.
9. Ibid.
10. Worldwatch Institute calculation based on Alan B. Durning and Holly B. Brough, *Taking Stock: Animal Farming and the Environment*, Worldwatch Paper 103 (Washington, D.C.: Worldwatch Institute, July 1991).
11. Data on grain exports from USDA, Foreign Agricultural Service (FAS), *World Grain Situation and Outlook*, Washington, D.C., August 1988; data on oil exports from British Petroleum, *BP Statistical Review of World Energy* (London: 1993).
12. USDA, ERS, *An Economic Analysis of USDA Erosion Control Programs* (Washington, D.C.: 1986); Gordon Sloggett and Clifford Dickason, *Ground-Water Mining in the United States* (Washington, D.C.: USDA, ERS, 1986).
13. Gary A. Margheim, *Implementing Conservation Compliance*

(Washington, D.C.: USDA, Soil Conservation Service, 1986); "Farmers Turn Down the Irrigation Tap," *Farmline*, August 1988; Sloggett and Dickason, op. cit. note 12.

14. U.N. Food and Agriculture Organization, *1992 Food Aid in Figures* (Rome: 1993).

15. Figure 2–3 is from Donald O. Mitchell and Merlinda D. Ingco, International Economics Department, *The World Food Outlook* (Washington, D.C.: World Bank, 1993).

16. World Bank, *World Development Report 1992* (New York: Oxford University Press, 1992); Table 2–1 is from UNDP, op. cit. note 1.

17. Table 2–2 is based on World Bank, unpublished printout, Washington, D.C., February 1992, on gross world product data for 1950 and 1955 from Herbert R. Block, *The Planetary Product in 1980: A Creative Pause?* (Washington, D.C.: U.S. Department of State, 1981), on Center for International Research, U.S. Bureau of the Census, Suitland, Md., private communication, March 26, 1993, and on International Monetary Fund (IMF), *World Economic Outlook: Interim Assessment* (Washington, D.C.: 1993).

18. World Bank, op. cit. note 16; Census Bureau, op. cit. note 17; IMF, op. cit. note 17.

19. UNDP, op. cit. note 1.

20. World Bank, op. cit. note 16; USDA, ERS, *Former USSR, Situation and Outlook Series*, Washington, D.C., May 1993; USDA, FAS, *World Grain Situation and Outlook*, Washington, D.C., September 1993.

21. Chicago Trade Board, op. cit. note 7.

CHAPTER 3. Ninety Million More

1. Center for International Research, U.S. Bureau of the Census, Suitland, Md., private communication, May 11, 1993, as revised.

2. Julius K. Nyerere, letter to Lester R. Brown, Dar es Salaam, Tanzania, June 26, 1975.

3. Lester R. Brown, *By Bread Alone* (New York: Praeger Publishers, 1974); Nyrere, op. cit. note 2.

4. Population Reference Bureau (PRB), *1993 World Population Data Sheet* (Washington, D.C.: 1993).

5. Centers for Disease Control, "Population Based Mortality Assessment: Baidoa and Afgoi, Somalia, 1992," *Journal of the American Medical Association*, January 6, 1993.

6. PRB, op. cit. note 4.

7. Ibid.; U.S. Department of Agriculture (USDA), Economic Re-

search Service (ERS), "World Grain Database" (unpublished printout), Washington, D.C., 1993; Sandra Postel, *Last Oasis: Facing Water Scarcity* (New York: W.W. Norton & Company, 1992).

8. Table 3–1 is from PRB, op. cit. note 4.
9. Figure 3–1 is from Census Bureau, op. cit. note 1; George Tseo, "The Greening of China," *Earthwatch*, May/June 1992.
10. Population numbers from Center for International Research, U.S. Bureau of the Census, Suitland, Md., private communication, November 2, 1993; Shiro Horiuchi, "Stagnation in the Decline of the World Population Growth Rate During the 1980s," *Science*, August 7, 1992.
11. Jodi L. Jacobson, "Abortion in a New Light," *World Watch*, March/April 1990.
12. The "demographic transition" is a term first used by Frank W. Notestein in 1945 in reference to the experience of Western Europe; it was later applied to the Third World; see Regina McNamara, "Demographic Transition Theory," *International Encyclopedia of Population*, Vol. 1 (New York: MacMillan Publishing Co., 1982).
13. Frank W. Notestein, Dudley Kirk, and Sheldon Segal, "The Problem of Population Control," in Philip M. Hauser, ed., *The Population Dilemma* (Englewood Cliffs, N.J.: Prentice Hall, Inc., 1963).
14. Ibid.
15. Figure 3–2 is from USDA, op. cit. note 7, and from USDA, Foreign Agricultural Service, *World Grain Situation and Outlook*, Washington, D.C., March 1993.
16. USDA, op. cit. note 15; population data from U.S. Bureau of the Census, published in Francis Urban and Ray Nightingale, *World Population by Country and Region, 1950–90 and Projections to 2050* (Washington, D.C.: USDA, ERS, 1993).
17. Table 3–2 is based on Census Bureau, op. cit. note 1.
18. Table 3–3 is from Urban and Nightingale, op. cit. note 16.
19. Ibid.
20. Horiuchi, op. cit. note 10.

CHAPTER 4. Climbing the Food Chain

1. Nicholas D. Kristof, "Riddle of China: Repression as Standard of Living Soars," *New York Times*, September 7, 1993.
2. U.N. Food and Agriculture Organization (FAO), *FAO Production Yearbook 1990* (Rome: 1991).
3. Table 4–1 is from ibid.
4. Ibid.

5. Production data, more readily available than consumption data, are used here for consumption. In reality, there are slight differences when the small trade in livestock products is taken into account, but these differences, where they exist, are typically so small that they are lost in the rounding to kilograms. Life expectancies from Population Reference Bureau (PRB), *1993 World Population Data Sheet* (Washington, D.C.: 1993).

6. Figure 4–1 is from FAO, *FAO Production Yearbook 1991* (Rome: 1992), from U.S. Department of Agriculture (USDA), *Dairy, Livestock and Poultry: World Livestock Situation*, Washington, D.C., October 1993, and from Center for International Research, U.S. Bureau of the Census, Suitland, Md., private communication, November 2, 1993.

7. Figure 4–2 is from FAO, op. cit. note 6, and from USDA, op cit. note 6.

8. Grain-to-beef conversion ratio based on Allen Baker, Feed Situation and Outlook Staff, Economic Research Service (ERS), USDA, Washington, D.C., private communication, April 27, 1992; pork conversion data from Leland Southard, Livestock and Poultry Situation and Outlook Staff, ERS, USDA, Washington, D.C., private communication April 27, 1992; feed-to-poultry conversion ratio derived from data in Robert V. Bishop et al., *The World Poultry Market — Government Intervention and Multilateral Policy Reform* (Washington, D.C.: USDA, 1990); fish conversion ratio from Ross Garnaut and Guonan Ma, East Asian Analytical Unit, Department of Foreign Affairs and Trade, *Grain In China* (Canberra: Australian Government Publishing Service, 1992); cheese and egg conversion ratios from Alan B. Durning and Holly B. Brough, *Taking Stock: Animal Farming and the Environment*, Worldwatch Paper 103 (Washington, D.C.: Worldwatch Institute, July 1991), citing USDA, Foreign Agricultural Service, *World Livestock Situation*, Washington, D.C., April 1991, and Linda Bailey, agricultural economist, USDA, Washington, D.C., private communication, September 11, 1990.

9. USDA, op. cit. note 6.

10. Durning and Brough, op. cit. note 8.

11. Figure 4–3 is from USDA, ERS, "Production, Supply, and Demand View" (electronic database), Washington, D.C., November 1993.

12. Figure 4–4 is from ibid.

13. USDA, Economic Research Service, *Western Europe Agriculture and Trade Situation and Outlook*, Washington, D.C., December 1992.

14. USDA, op. cit. note 11.
15. Ibid.
16. USDA, *Agricultural Statistics 1992* (Washington D.C.: U.S. Government Printing Office, 1992).
17. USDA, "World Soybean Database" (unpublished printout), Washington, D.C., 1992.
18. USDA, "World Oilseed Database" (unpublished printout), Washington, D.C., 1991; USDA, *World Oilseed Situation and Outlook Report*, Washington, D.C., February 1993.
19. FAO, *1992 Food Aid in Figures* (Rome: 1993).
20. PRB, op. cit. note 5.

CHAPTER 5. Overharvesting the Oceans

1. Victoria Griffith, "Too Few Fish in the Sea," *Financial Times*, May 27, 1992; Lawrence Ingrassia, "Overfishing Threatens To Wipe Out Species and Crush Industry," *Wall Street Journal*, July 16, 1991; David Blackwell, "Ban on Industrial Fishing Called For," *Financial Times*, June 23, 1992; Bernard Simon, "Canada Set to Impose Ban on Atlantic Cod Fishing," *Financial Times*, July 2, 1992.
2. Anne Swardson, "Canada Closes Section of Atlantic to Fishing," *Washington Post*, September 1, 1993; Christopher B. Daly, "Fishermen Beached As Harvest Dries Up," *Washington Post*, March 3, 1994.
3. "Salmon Fishing Banned Along Washington Coast," *Los Angeles Times*, as reprinted in *Washington Post*, April 10, 1994.
4. U.N. Food and Agriculture Organization (FAO), Fishery Information, Data, and Statistics Service (FIDI), Rome, private communications, various dates.
5. Figure 5-1 is from FAO, *Yearbook of Fishery Statistics: Catches and Landings* (Rome: various years) and from FAO, Rome, private communications, December 20, 1993.
6. FAO, *The State of Food and Agriculture 1993* (Rome: 1993).
7. Ingrassia, op. cit. note 1.
8. FAO, cited in World Resources Institute (WRI), *World Resources 1992–93* (New York: Oxford University Press, 1992); bluefin tuna figure from Donella Meadows et al., *Beyond the Limits* (Post Mills, Vt.: Chelsea Green Publishing Company, 1992).
9. Simon, op. cit. note 1.
10. Mike Griffin, "Some Very Fishy Business," *South*, August 1991; "Minister Says Fishing Policies Beginning To Show Results," *Environmental Issues*, May 22, 1992.
11. Table 5-1 is from FAO, "World Apparent Consumption Statis-

tics Based on Food Balance Sheets (1961–89)," *FAO Fisheries Circular No. 821*, Rome, July 1991.

12. Lester Brown, "The Aral Sea: Going, Going. . .," *World Watch*, January/February 1991; Environment and Urban Affairs Division, Government of Pakistan, and IUCN–The World Conservation Union, *The Pakistan National Conservation Strategy* (Karachi: 1992); Government of Canada, *The State of Canada's Environment* (Ottawa, 1991).

13. Tom Horton and William M. Eichbaum, *Turning the Tide: Saving the Chesapeake Bay* (Washington, D.C.: Island Press, 1991); Government of Canada, op. cit. note 12.

14. Figure 5–2 is a Worldwatch calculation based on 100 million tons of seafood and on data from the U.S. Bureau of the Census, private communication, unpublished printout, March 26, 1993.

15. FAO, "Aquaculture Production 1984–1990," *FAO Fisheries Circular No. 815 Revision 4*, Rome, June 1992; 1992 figure is Worldwatch estimate.

16. FAO, op. cit. note 8.

17. Ibid.

18. Testimony of Dr. Susan Weiler, Executive Director, American Society of Limnology and Oceanography, Department of Biology, Whitman College, Walla Walla, Wash., before Hearing on Global Change Research: Ozone Depletion and Its Impacts, U.S. Senate, Committee on Commerce, Science, and Transportation, Washington, D.C., November 15, 1991.

19. Foy quoted in Ingrassia, op. cit. note 1.

20. Food from better cleaning from Michael Satchell, "The Rape of the Oceans," *U.S. News and World Report*, June 22, 1992.

21. Robert Walters, "Aquaculture Catches On," *Mt. Vernon Register News*, July 31, 1987; grain-to-beef conversion ratio based on Allen Baker, Feed Situation and Outlook Staff, Economic Research Service (ERS), U.S. Department of Agriculture (USDA), Washington, D.C., private communication, April 27, 1992; pork conversion ratio from Leland Southard, Livestock and Poultry Situation and Outlook Staff, ERS, USDA, Washington, D.C., private communication, April 27, 1992; feed-to-poultry conversion ratio derived from data in Robert V. Bishop et al., *The World Poultry Market—Government Intervention and Multilateral Policy Reform* (Washington, D.C.: USDA, 1990), from Linda Bailey, Livestock and Poultry Situation Staff, ERS, USDA, Washington,D.C., private communication, April 27, 1992, and from various issues of *Feedstuffs*.

22. Figure 5–3 is from FAO, *Yearbook of Fishery Statistics: Catches and Landings* (Rome: 1993), from FAO, "Aquaculture Produc-

tion 1985–1991," *FAO Fisheries Circular No. 815 Revision 5,* Rome, June 1993, and from FAO, op. cit. note 15.

23. Tim Coone, "Salmon Farms Blamed for Parasite Problem," *Financial Times,* August 6, 1992; Caroline E. Mayer, "Caught Up in a Salmon Rivalry," *Washington Post,* April 24, 1991; James Buxton, " 'Cowboy' Salmon Farmers Come Under Fire," *Financial Times,* January 30, 1991.

24. Price data and Figure 5–4 are from U.S. Department of Labor, Bureau of Labor Statistics, "Consumer Price Index" (unpublished printout), Washington, D.C., October 2, 1992, and April 21, 1994.

25. USDA, ERS, "Red Meat, Poultry, and Fish (Boneless, Trimmed Equivalent): Per Capita Consumption, 1967–89," Washington, D.C., private communication, January 15, 1991.

26. FAO, *The State of Food and Agriculture 1989* (Rome: 1989); David Blackwell, "EC Fish Deficit Widens as Demand Increases," *Financial Times,* September 3, 1992; FAO, *Yearbook of Fishery Statistics: Catches and Landings* (Rome: 1992).

27. FAO, Rome, private communication, March 23, 1993; meat from FAO, *FAO Production Yearbook* (Rome: various years), and from USDA, *World Agricultural Production,* August and September 1991.

CHAPTER 6. Overgrazing Rangelands

1. Land area statistics from U.N. Food and Agriculture Organization (FAO), *FAO Production Yearbook 1992* (Rome: 1993); Table 6–1 is from FAO, *FAO Production Yearbook 1991* (Rome: 1992); FAO, *1948–1985 World Crop and Livestock Statistics* (Rome: 1987).

2. FAO, *Production Yearbook 1992,* op. cit. note 1.

3. Ibid.

4. U.S. Department of Agriculture (USDA), *Dairy, Livestock, and Poultry: World Livestock Situation,* Washington, D.C., October 1993.

5. Figure 6–1 is from ibid.

6. Alan B. Durning and Holly B. Brough, *Taking Stock: Animal Farming and the Environment,* Worldwatch Paper 103 (Washington, D.C.: Worldwatch Institute, July 1991).

7. FAO, *1948–1985 Statistics,* op. cit. note 1; FAO, *Production Yearbooks* (Rome: various years); USDA, *World Agricultural Production* (Washington, D.C.: U.S. Government Printing Office (GPO), various years).

8. Edward C. Wolf, "Managing Rangelands," in Lester R. Brown

et al., *State of the World 1986* (New York: W.W. Norton & Company, 1986); African livestock data for 1950 from FAO, *FAO Production Yearbook 1954* (Rome: 1955), and for 1987 from *FAO Production Yearbook 1987* (Rome: 1988); population from Population Reference Bureau, *1992 World Population Data Sheet* (Washington, D.C.: 1992).

9. FAO, *Production Yearbook 1987*, op. cit. note 8; Southern African Development Coordination Conference, *SADCC Agriculture: Toward 2000* (Rome: FAO, 1984).

10. Wolf, op. cit. note 8; Government of India, "Strategies, Structures, Policies: National Wastelands Development Board," New Delhi, mimeographed, February 6, 1986; M.V. Desai, "Gujarat: Lending Helping Hand," *Hindustan Times* (New Delhi), October 8, 1988.

11. USDA, *Agricultural Statistics 1990* (Washington, D.C.: GPO, 1990); Table 6–2 is from H. Dregne et al. "A New Assessment of the World Status of Desertification," *Desertification Control Bulletin*, No. 20, 1991.

12. Dregne et al., op. cit. note 11.

13. USDA, op. cit. note 4.

CHAPTER 7. Limits of the Plow

1. U.S. Department of Agriculture (USDA), Economic Research Service (ERS), "Production, Supply, and Demand View" (electronic database), Washington, D.C., November 1993.

2. Figure 7–1 from ibid., with data for 1950–59 from USDA, ERS, "World Grain Database" (unpublished printout), Washington, D.C., 1992.

3. USDA, op. cit. note 1.

4. Lester R. Brown and John Young, "Feeding the World in the Nineties," in Lester R. Brown et al., *State of the World 1990* (New York: W.W. Norton & Company, 1990).

5. USDA, op. cit. note 1; USDA, *World Grain Situation and Outlook*, Washington, D.C., April 1993; Soviet area from USDA, ERS, *Former USSR, Situation and Outlook Series*, Washington, D.C., May 1993; Conservation Reserve Program land area from USDA, ERS, Resources and Technology Division, *RTD UPDATES: 1993 Cropland Use*, Washington, D.C., September 1993.

6. USDA, *RTD UPDATES*, op. cit. note 5; European land set-aside from Dan Plunkett, USDA, Washington, D.C., private communication, October 20, 1993.

7. USDA, op. cit. note 1; United Nations, *World Economic Survey*

1991 (New York: 1991); Norimitsu Onishi, "Japanese Pass US Automakers In Race for Chinese Ventures," *Journal of Comerce*, August 31, 1993; Population Reference Bureau (PRB), *1993 World Population Data Sheet* (Washington, D.C.: 1993); USDA, op. cit. note 2.

8. David E. Dowall, "The Land Market Assessment: A New Tool for Urban Management," paper prepared for the Urban Management Program of United Nations Center for Human Settlements, World Bank, and United Nations Development Programme, University of California, Berkeley, March 1991; PRB, op. cit. note 7.

9. Annual population increase from Center for International Research, U.S. Bureau of the Census, Suitland, Md., private communication, March 26, 1993; grain equivalent of parking 100 cars calculated using yield data from USDA, op. cit. note 1; quote from M. Rupert Cutler, "The Peril of Vanishing Farmlands," *New York Times*, July 1, 1980.

10. Elizabeth Checchio, *Water Farming: The Promise and Problems of Water Transfers in Arizona* (Tucson: University of Arizona, 1988); Sandra Postel, *Last Oasis: Facing Water Scarcity* (New York: W.W. Norton & Company, 1992).

11. Figure 7–2 is from USDA, op. cit. note 1.

12. Ibid.

13. Ibid.

14. Census Bureau, op. cit. note 9; Figure 7–3 is based on U.S. Bureau of the Census, published in Francis Urban and Ray Nightingale, *World Population by Country and Region, 1950–90 and Projections to 2050* (Washington, D.C.: USDA, ERS, 1993), and on USDA, op. cit. note 1.

15. Table 7–1 based on Census Bureau, op. cit. note 9, and on Urban and Nightingale, op. cit. note 14.

CHAPTER 8. Spreading Water Scarcity

1. Joseph A. Tainter, *The Collapse of Complex Societies* (New York: Cambridge University Press, 1988).

2. Figure 8–1 is from U.N. Food and Agriculture Organization (FAO), *Production Yearbook 1990* (Rome: 1991), and from Bill Quimby, Economic Research Service (ERS), U.S. Department of Agriculture (USDA), Washington, D.C., private communication, March 20, 1992; per capita figures based on population data from Center for International Research, U.S. Bureau of the Census, Suitland, Md., private communication, March 26, 1993.

3. Figure 8–2 is from FAO, op. cit. note 2, from Quimby, op. cit. note 2, and from Census Bureau, op. cit. note 2.

4. World Bank, *World Development Report 1982* (New York: Oxford University Press, 1982); Gordon Sloggett and Clifford Dickason, *Ground-Water Mining in the United States* (Washington, D.C.: USDA, ERS, 1986); Ashok V. Desai, "The Indian Electric Power System," *Economic and Political Weekly*, October 10, 1987; B.D. Dhawan, "Management of Groundwater Resource: Direct Versus Indirect Regulatory Mechanisms," *Economic and Political Weekly*, September 5–12, 1987.

5. FAO, op. cit. note 2; USDA, ERS, *Agricultural Resources: Cropland, Water and Conservation Situation and Outlook Report*, Washington, D.C., September 1991.

6. Table 8–1 is from FAO, op. cit. note 2, and from USDA, op. cit. note 5; Frederick W. Crook, *Agricultural Statistics of the People's Republic of China, 1949–86* (Washington, D.C.: USDA, ERS, 1988).

7. Center for Monitoring the Indian Economy, Economic Intelligence Service, *Basic Statistics Relating to the Indian Economy, Vol. 1: All India* (Bombay: 1984).

8. FAO, *Production Yearbook* (Rome: various years); Sloggett and Dickason, op. cit. note 4; Sandra Postel, *Water: Rethinking Management in an Age of Scarcity*, Worldwatch Paper 62 (Washington, D.C.: Worldwatch Institute, December 1984); USDA, ERS, *USSR: Agriculture and Trade Report*, Washington, D.C., May 1988.

9. Sandra Postel, *Last Oasis: Facing Water Scarcity* (New York: W.W. Norton & Company, 1992), citing M.G. Chandrakanth and Jeff Romm, "Groundwater Depletion in India—Institutional Management Regimes," *Natural Resources Journal*, Summer 1990, and U.S Geological Survey, *Estimated Water Use of the United States in 1990* (Washington, D.C.: U.S. Government Printing Office, 1992).

10. USDA, "Production, Supply, and Demand View" (electronic database), Washington, D.C., November 1993.

11. Amu Darya flow from Phillip P. Micklin, *The Water Management Crisis in Soviet Central Asia*, The Carl Beck Papers in Russian and East European Studies (Pittsburgh, Pa.: University of Pittsburgh, 1991); Colorado and Huang He flows from Postel, op. cit. note 9.

12. FAO, *FAO Production Yearbook 1986* (Rome: 1987); Sloggett and Dickason, op. cit. note 4; Postel, op. cit. note 8.

13. Daniel P. Beard, "Blueprint for Reform: The Commissioner's Plan for Reinventing Reclamation," Bureau of Reclamation,

U.S. Department of Interior, Washington, D.C., November 1993.

14. Sloggett and Dickason, op. cit. note 4.

15. Chinese irrigated area fell from 45 million hectares in 1977 to 40 million hectares in 1985, according to Crook, op. cit. note 6; Li Rongxia, "Irrigation System in Central Shaanxi," *Beijing Review*, December 14–20, 1987; Nie Lisheng, "State Organizes Farmers to Work on Irrigation," *China Daily*, January 16, 1988.; David Fraser, "Water Crisis Threatens to Dry Up China's Future," *New Straits Times*, May 8, 1986; Postel, op. cit. note 8; Sloggett and Dickason, op. cit. note 4.

16. Niu quoted in Patrick E. Tyler, "China Lacks Water to Meet Its Mighty Thirst," *New York Times*, November 7, 1993; People's Republic of China, State Science and Technology Commission, *Beijing-Tianjin Water Resources Study: Final Report* (Beijing: 1991).

17. Salamat Ali, "Adrift in Flood and Drought," *Far Eastern Economic Review*, August 27, 1987; Navin C. Joshi, "Ground Water Crisis Swells Up," *Business Standard*, April 26, 1988; B.B. Vohra, *When Minor Becomes Major: Some Problems of Ground Water Management* (New Dehli: Advisory Board on Energy, 1986).

18. R.P.S. Malik and Paul Faeth, "Rice-Wheat Production in Northwest India," in Paul Faeth, ed., *Agricultural Policy and Sustainability: Case Studies from India, Chile, the Philippines, and the United States* (Washington, D.C.: World Resources Institute, 1993).

19. David Seckler, "World Grain Consumption and Production: 1961–2030" (draft), Washington, D.C., Winrock Center for Economic Policy Studies, November 1993.

20. Postel, op. cit. note 9.

21. Lester R. Brown, "The Aral Sea: Going, Going. . .," *World Watch*, January/February 1991.

22. Ibid.

23. Ibid.

24. Ibid.

25. Ibid.

26. Ibid.

27. Elizabeth Checchio, *Water Farming: The Promise and Problems of Water Transfers in Arizona* (Tucson: University of Arizona, 1988); People's Republic of China, op. cit. note 16.

28. From Postel, op. cit. note 9, citing Richard W. Wahl, *Markets for Federal Water: Subsidies, Property Rights, and the Bureau of Reclamation* (Washington, D.C.: Resources for the Future, 1989),

and World Bank, *India: Irrigation Sector Review,* Vol. 1 (Washington D.C.: 1991).

29. Drip irrigation from J.S. Abbot, "Micro Irrigation—World Wide Usage," *ICID Bulletin,* January 1984; intermittent flooding from D. Tabbal, R. Lampayan, and S.I. Bhuiyan, "Water Saving Irrigation Technique for Rice," presented at the International Workshop on Soil and Water Engineering for Paddy Field Management Agricultural Land and Water Development Program, Asian Institute of Technology, Bangkok, Thailand, January 28–30, 1992.

CHAPTER 9. The Fertilizer Falloff

1. "Justus von Liebig," *Encyclopaedia Britannica* (Cambridge: Encyclopaedia Britannica, Inc., 1976).
2. U.S. Department of Agriculture (USDA), Economic Research Service (ERS), "World Grain Database" (unpublished printout), Washington, D.C., October 1993.
3. Figure 9–1 is from U.N. Food and Agriculture Organization (FAO), *FAO Production Yearbooks* (Rome: various years), from FAO, *Fertilizer Yearbooks* (Rome: various years), and from International Fertilizer Industry Association (IFA), *Fertilizer Consumption Report* (Paris: 1992).
4. For declining response to fertilizer, see Duane Chapman and Randy Barker, *Resource Depletion, Agricultural Research, and Development* (Ithaca, N.Y.: Cornell University, 1987); USDA, *USSR Agriculture and Trade Report,* Washington, D.C., May 1991; IFA, *Fertilizer Consumption Report* (Paris: 1993).
5. Figure 9–2 is from FAO, *Production Yearbooks,* op. cit. note 3, from FAO, *Fertilizer Yearbooks,* op. cit. note 3, and from IFA, op. cit. note 3.
6. Lester R. Brown and Jodi Jacobson, "Assessing the Future of Urbanization," in Lester R. Brown et al., *State of the World 1987* (New York: W.W. Norton & Company, 1987), citing Robert K. Bastian and Jay Benforado, "Waste Treatment: Doing What Comes Naturally," *Technology Review,* February/March 1983.
7. Export figure from USDA, op. cit. note 2.
8. Figure 9–3 is from FAO, *Fertilizer Yearbooks,* op. cit. note 3, and from IFA, op. cit. note 3.
9. FAO, *Production Yearbooks,* op. cit. note 3; FAO, *Fertilizer Yearbooks,* op. cit. note 3; IFA, op. cit. note 3; Center for International Research, U.S. Bureau of the Census, Suitland, Md., private communication, November 2, 1993.

10. IFA, op. cit. note 3.
11. "Fritz Haber" and "Carl Bosch," *Encyclopaedia Britannica* (Cambridge: Encyclopaedia Britannica, Inc., 1976).
12. Brown and Jacobson, op. cit. note 6, citing Yue-Man Yeung, "Urban Agriculture in Asia," The Food Energy Nexus Programme of the United Nations University, Tokyo, September 1985.
13. Figure 9–4 is from FAO, *Production Yearbooks*, op. cit. note 3, from FAO, *Fertilizer Yearbooks*, op. cit. note 3, and from IFA, op. cit. note 3.
14. USDA, op. cit. note 4; IFA, op. cit. note 3.
15. USDA, *China: Agricultural and Trade Report*, Washington, D.C., various issues; IFA, op. cit. note 3; FAO, *Fertilizer Yearbooks*, op. cit. note 3.
16. Figure 9–5 is from USDA, op. cit. note 4, and from IFA, op. cit. note 3.
17. "Fertilizer Firms' Hopes for Turnaround are Frustrated," *Wall Street Journal*, December 11, 1992; Ashok Gulati and G.D. Kalra, "Fertilizer Subsidy: Issues Related to Efficiency," *Economic and Political Weekly*, March 28, 1992.
18. USDA, ERS, "Production, Supply, and Demand View" (electronic database), Washington, D.C., November 1993.
19. K.F. Isherwood and K.G. Soh, "Short Term Prospects for World Agriculture and Fertilizer Use," IFA, Paris, November 1993.
20. Table 9–1 is from FAO, *Fertilizer Yearbooks*, op. cit. note 3, from IFA, op. cit. note 3, from USDA, op. cit. note 2, and from USDA, op. cit. note 18.
21. FAO, *Fertilizer Yearbooks*, op. cit. note 3; IFA, op. cit. note 3; USDA, op. cit. note 2.
22. Chapman and Barker, op. cit. note 4.
23. USDA, op. cit. note 4; IFA, op. cit. note 3; Isherwood and Soh,. op. cit. note 19.
24. Isherwood and Soh, op. cit. note 19.

CHAPTER 10. Struggling to Raise Yields

1. Figure 10–1 is from historical data in Lester R. Brown, *Man, Land, and Food* (Washington, D.C.: U.S. Department of Agriculture (USDA), 1963), and from data since 1950 in USDA, Economic Research Service (ERS), "World Grain Database" (unpublished printout), Washington, D.C., 1992.
2. Historical data from Brown, op. cit. note 1; data since 1950 from USDA, op. cit. note 1.

3. Figure 10–2 is from USDA, op. cit. note 1.
4. Figure 10–3 and other nations' yields are from USDA, op. cit. note 1; irrigated area figures from "Thirsty Fields: Asia's Rice Lands," *AsiaWeek*, May 26, 1993.
5. USDA, op. cit. note 1; Duane Chapman and Randy Barker, *Resource Depletion, Agricultural Research, and Development* (Ithaca, N.Y.: Cornell University, 1987).
6. Figure 10–4 is from USDA, op. cit. note 1.
7. Prabhu L. Pingali, International Rice Research Institute, and Mark W. Rosegrant, International Food Policy Research Institute, "Confronting the Environmental Consequences of the Green Revolution in Asia," presented at 1993 AAEA International Pre-Conference on Post-Green Revolution Agricultural Development Strategies in the Third World: What Next?, August 1993.
8. Ibid.
9. Ibid.
10. Robert W. Herdt, "Technological Potential for Increasing Crop Productivity in Developing Countries," paper presented to the meeting of the International Trade Research Consortium, December 14–18, 1986.
11. Figure 10–5 is from USDA, op. cit. note 1.
12. Donald N. Duvick, "Intensification of Known Technology and Prospects of Breakthroughs in Technology and Future Food Supply," Iowa State University, Johnston, Iowa, February 1994.
13. Ibid.
14. Ibid.
15. United Nations, *World Population Prospects, The 1992 Revision* (New York: 1993); Population Reference Bureau, *1993 World Population Data Sheet* (Washington, D.C.: 1993).
16. USDA, ERS, "Production, Supply, and Demand View" (electronic database), Washington, D.C., November 1993.
17. Donald O. Mitchell and Merlinda D. Ingco, International Economics Department, *The World Food Outlook* (Washington, D.C.: World Bank, November 1993); USDA, op. cit. note 16.
18. Possible influence of higher prices from Donald L. Plucknett, "Science and Agricultural Transformation," International Food Policy Research Institute Lecture Series, No. 1, Washington, D.C., September 1993.
19. USDA, op. cit. note 1.
20. Figure 10–6 is from Henrich von Loesch, Information Services,

Consultative Group on International Agricultural Research, private communication, April 7, 1994.
21. Mitchell and Ingco, op. cit. note 17.

CHAPTER 11. Environmental Deductions

1. Josef R. Parrington et al., "Asian Dust: Seasonal Transport to the Hawaiian Islands," *Science*, April 8, 1983.
2. Ken Newcombe, *An Economic Justification for Rural Afforestation: The Case of Ethiopia*, Energy Department Paper No. 16 (Washington, D.C.: World Bank, 1984).
3. Ibid.
4. United Nations Development Programme/World Bank Energy Sector Assessment Program, *Ethiopia: Issues and Options in the Energy Sector* (Washington, D.C.: World Bank, 1984); Kenneth Newcombe, "Household Energy Supply: The Energy Crisis That is Here to Stay!" presented to the World Bank Senior Policy Seminar—Energy, Gabarone, Botswana, March 18–22, 1985.
5. Share of land that is dryland from U.S. Department of Agriculture (USDA), *Agricultural Statistics 1990* (Washington, D.C.: U.S. Government Printing Office (GPO), 1990); Table 11–1 is from H. Dregne et al., "A New Assessment of the World Status of Desertification," *Desertification Control Bulletin*, No. 20, 1991.
6. Dregne et al., op. cit. note 5.
7. Lester R. Brown, *The Changing World Food Prospect: The Nineties and Beyond*, Worldwatch Paper 85 (Washington, D.C.: Worldwatch Institute, October 1988); Leon Lyles, "Possible Effects of Wind Erosion on Soil Productivity," *Journal of Soil and Water Conservation*, November/December 1975.
8. World Bank, *World Development Report 1992* (New York: Oxford University Press, 1992); Jason W. Clay et al., *The Spoils of Famine: Ethiopian Famine Policy and Peasant Agriculture* (Cambridge, Mass: Cultural Survival, Inc., 1988); USDA, Economic Research Service (ERS), "Production, Supply, and Demand View" (electronic database), Washington, D.C., November 1993; USDA, ERS, *Agricultural Resources: Cropland, Water, and Conservation Situation and Outlook Report*, Washington, D.C., September 1991.
9. Sandra Postel, *Last Oasis: Facing Water Scarcity* (New York: W.W. Norton & Company, 1992).

10. K. Mahmood, *Reservoir Sedimentation: Impact, Extent, and Mitigation*, World Bank Technical Paper No. 71 (Washington, D.C.: World Bank, 1987).
11. Clay et al., op. cit. note 8.
12. Barbara J. Cummings, *Dam the Rivers, Damn the People* (London: World Wildlife Fund and Earthscan Publications, Ltd., 1990).
13. "Forests, Crops Suffering Ozone Damage," *Dagens Nyheter*, July 5, 1990, as reprinted in *JPRS Report: Environmental Issues*, October 12, 1990; Dr. Jan Cerovsky, "Environmental Status Report 1988/89: Czechoslovakia," in World Conservation Union—IUCN, *Environmental Status Reports: 1988/89, Vol. 1: Czechoslovakia, Hungary, Poland* (Thatcham, U.K.: Thatcham Printers, 1990).
14. James J. MacKenzie and Mohamed T. El-Ashry, *Ill Winds: Airborne Pollution's Toll on Trees and Crops* (Washington, D.C.: World Resources Institute, 1988); National Acid Precipitation Assessment Program, *Interim Assessment: The Causes and Effects of Acid Deposition*, Vol. IV (Washington, D.C.: GPO, 1987); economic loss estimated by Walter W. Heck, chairman, Research Committee, National Crop Loss Assessment Network, cited in MacKenzie and El-Ashry, op. cit. in this note.
15. Enquete Commission of the German Bundestag (ed.), *Climate Change—A Threat to Global Development* (Bonn and Karlsruhe: Economica Verlag and Verlag C.F. Muller, 1992); MacKenzie and El-Ashry, op. cit. note 14.
16. Alan H. Teramura, Professor and Chairman, Department of Botany, University of Maryland, College Park, Testimony to the U.S. Senate Hearing on Global Change Research: Ozone Depletion and its Impacts, November 15, 1991.
17. Ibid.
18. Ibid.; "Increased Ultraviolet Radiation Stunts Rice Plant Growth," International Rice Research Institute, News Release, Manila, Philippines, December 1991.
19. Teramura, op. cit. note 16; "Scientists Say Ozone Depletion Could Affect Productivity of Plants," *International Environment Reporter*, April 22, 1992; Dr. Susan Weiler, Executive Director, American Society of Limnology and Oceanography, Department of Biology, Whitman College, Walla Walla, Wash., Testimony to the U.S. Senate Hearing on Global Change Research: Ozone Depletion and its Impacts, Washington, D.C., November 15, 1991.

20. Weiler, op. cit. note 19.
21. James E. Hansen, "The Greenhouse Effect: Impacts on Current Global Temperature and Regional Heat Waves," statement before the Committee on Energy and Natural Resources, U.S. Senate, Washington, D.C., June 23, 1988, and as quoted in Michael Weisskopf, " 'Greenhouse Effect' Fueling Policy Makers," *Washington Post*, August 15, 1988; Syukuro Manabe, "Climate Warming Due to Greenhouse Gases," statement before the Subcommittee on Toxic Substances and Environmental Oversight, U.S. Senate, Washington, D.C., December 10, 1985; J. Hansen et al., "Global Climate Changes as Forecast by the GISS 3-D Model," *Journal of Geophysical Research*, August 1988.
22. Hansen, op. cit. note 21; USDA, ERS, "World Grain Harvested Area, Production, and Yield 1950–87" (unpublished printout), Washington, D.C., 1988.
23. Hansen, op. cit. note 21.
24. Ibid.
25. Sandra Postel, *Water for Agriculture: Facing the Limits*, Worldwatch Paper 93 (Washington, D.C.: Worldwatch Institute, December 1989).
26. Paul R. Ehrlich, Anne H. Ehrlich, and Gretchen C. Daily, "Food Security, Population, and Environment," *Population and Development Review*, March 1993.
27. Cynthia Rosenzweig and Martin L. Parry, "Potential Impact of Climate Change on World Food Supply," *Nature*, January 13, 1994.
28. Ibid.

CHAPTER 12. Carrying Capacity: The Big Four

1. Slowing growth in grain yields from U.S. Department of Agriculture (USDA), Economic Research Service (ERS), "Production, Supply, and Demand View" (electronic database), Washington, D.C., November 1993.
2. Population data from Center for International Research, U.S. Bureau of the Census, Suitland, Md., private communication, November 2, 1993.
3. Ibid.
4. Donald N. Duvick, "Intensification of Known Technology and Prospects of Breakthroughs in Technology and Future Food Supply," Iowa State University, Johnston, Iowa, February 1994.

5. Donald O. Mitchell and Merlinda D. Ingco, International Economics Department, *The World Food Outlook* (Washington, D.C.: World Bank, November 1993); Nikos Alexandros, "The Outlook for World Food and Agriculture to the Year 2010," U.N. Food and Agriculture Organization (FAO), Rome, February 1994.

6. Population numbers from U.S. Bureau of the Census, published in Francis Urban and Ray Nightingale, *World Population by Country and Region, 1950–90 and Projections to 2050* (Washington, D.C.: USDA, ERS, 1993); consumption projection is Worldwatch calculation based on USDA, op. cit. note 1.

7. Table 12–1 is from USDA, op. cit. note 1, with production figures for 1950–60 from USDA, ERS, "World Grain Database" (unpublished printout), Washington, D.C., 1992.

8. Return of cropland to planting from USDA, ERS, *Agricultural Resources: Cropland, Water, and Conservation Situation and Outlook Report*, Washington, D.C., September 1991.

9. Table 12–2 is from USDA, op. cit. note 1, from USDA, op. cit. note 7, from Urban and Nightingale, op. cit. note 6, and from FAO, *Production Yearbook 1950* (Rome: 1951) for 1950 trade figures.

10. USDA, op. cit. note 1.

11. Ibid.

12. Ibid.

13. Per capita grain area from USDA, op. cit. note 1, and from USDA, op. cit. note 7; water scarcity from Sandra Postel, *Last Oasis: Facing Water Scarcity* (New York: W.W. Norton & Company, 1992).

14. FAO, *Production Yearbook 1992* (Rome: 1993).

15. Lester R. Brown, *The Changing World Food Prospect: The Nineties and Beyond*, Worldwatch Paper 85 (Washington, D.C., Worldwatch Institute, October 1988).

16. Yields from USDA, op. cit. note 1; fertilizer use from K.F. Isherwood and K.G. Soh, "Short Term Prospects for World Agriculture and Fertilizer Use," International Fertilizer Association, Paris, November 1993.

17. USDA, op. cit. note 1.

18. Ibid.

19. Quoted in Patrick E. Tyler, "The Dynamic New China Still Races Against Time," *New York Times*, January 2, 1994.

20. USDA, op. cit. note 1; Urban and Nightingale, op. cit. note 6.

21. Production figures from USDA, op. cit. note 1, and from USDA, op. cit. note 7; USDA, *USSR: Agriculture and Trade Report*, Washington, D.C., May 1988; Lester R. Brown, "The

Aral Sea: Going, Going. . .," *World Watch*, January/February 1991.
22. USDA, op. cit. note 21.

CHAPTER 13. Carrying Capacity: The Next Nine

1. U.S. Bureau of the Census, published in Francis Urban and Ray Nightingale, *World Population by Country and Region, 1950–90 and Projections to 2050* (Washington, D.C.: U.S. Department of Agriculture (USDA), Economic Research Service (ERS), 1993); USDA, ERS, "Production, Supply, and Demand View" (electronic database), Washington, D.C., November 1993; Sandra Postel, *Last Oasis: Facing Water Scarcity* (New York: W.W. Norton & Company, 1992).
2. U.N. Food and Agriculture Organization (FAO), *FAO Production Yearbook 1991* (Rome: 1992).
3. Table 13–1 from USDA, op. cit. note 1, with production figures for 1950–60 from USDA, ERS, "World Grain Database" (unpublished printout), Washington, D.C., 1992, from FAO, *Production Yearbook 1950* (Rome: 1951), and from Urban and Nightingale, op. cit. note 1; decline in rice yields from USDA, op. cit. note 1.
4. Share irrigated and waterlogging and salting problems from Postel, op. cit. note 1.
5. Environment and Urban Affairs Division, Government of Pakistan, and IUCN–The World Conservation Union, *The Pakistan National Conservation Strategy* (Karachi: 1992).
6. Population numbers from Urban and Nightingale, op. cit. note 1; irrigation from FAO, *Production Yearbook 1992* (Rome: 1993).
7. World Resources Institute, *World Resources 1994–95* (New York: Oxford University Press, 1994).
8. Composition of grain harvest from USDA, op. cit. note 1.
9. Food aid information from FAO, *1993 State of Food and Agriculture* (Rome: 1993).
10. Principal crops from USDA, op. cit. note 1.

CHAPTER 14. The Growing Imbalance

1. Worldwatch projections based on U.S. Department of Agriculture (USDA), Economic Research Service (ERS), "World Grain Database" (unpublished printout), Washington, D.C., 1992, on USDA, "Production, Supply, and Demand View" (electronic database), Washington, D.C., November 1993, and

on U.S. Bureau of the Census, published in Ray Urban and Francis Nightingale, *World Population by Country and Region, 1950–1990, and Projections to 2050* (Washington, D.C.: USDA, ERS, 1993).
2. Annual increment from USDA, "Production, Supply, and Demand View," op. cit. note 1.
3. Ibid.
4. Ibid.
5. Peter Hazell, "Prospects for a Well Fed World" (draft), International Food Policy Research Institute, Washington, D.C., March 1994.
6. Ibid.
7. Population increase from Urban and Nightingale, op. cit. note 1.
8. U.N. Food and Agriculture Organization (FAO), *Fertilizer Yearbook* (Rome: 1993).
9. Table 14–1 is based on FAO, *Yearbook of Fishery Statistics: Catches and Landings* (Rome: 1993), on USDA, "World Grain Database," op. cit. note 1, and on USDA, "Production, Supply, and Demand View," op. cit. note 1.
10. Hazell, op. cit. note 5.
11. U.S. Department of Labor, Bureau of Labor Statistics, "Consumer Price Index" (unpublished printout), Washington, D.C., April 13, 1994.
12. Rice prices from Chicago Trade Board, private communication, November 1993.
13. Grain price doubling in 1972–73 from International Money Fund, *International Financial Statistics Yearbook: Historical Edition* (Washington, D.C.: 1979).
14. USDA, "World Grain Database," op. cit. note 1.
15. Hal Kane, "Overall Cigarette Production Rises," in Lester R. Brown, Hal Kane, and David Malin Roodman, *Vital Signs 1994* (New York: W.W. Norton & Company, 1994).
16. United Nations Development Programme, *Human Development Report 1993* (New York: Oxford University Press, 1993).
17. John Cogan, Energy Information Administration, U.S Department of Energy, Washington, D.C., private communication, February 24, 1994.
18. Number of Indian farmers from World Bank, *Social Indicators of Development 1993* (Baltimore, Md.: Johns Hopkins University Press, 1993).
19. USDA, *Dairy, Livestock and Poultry: World Livestock Situation*, Washington, D.C., October 1993.
20. Conversion figure for beef and mutton from Allen Baker, Feed Situation and Outlook Staff, USDA, ERS, Washington, D.C.,

private communication, April 27, 1992; conversion figure for fish from Ross Garnaut and Guonan Ma, East Asian Analytical Unit, Department of Foreign Affairs and Trade, *Grain in China* (Canberra: Australian Government Publishing Service, 1992).
21. Consumption figures from FAO, *FAO Production Yearbook 1992* (Rome: 1993).

CHAPTER 15. Reassessing Population Policy

1. U.N. Food and Agriculture Organization (FAO), *Fishery Statistics: Catches and Landings* (Rome: 1992); Center for International Research, U.S. Bureau of the Census, Suitland, Md., private communication, November 2, 1993.
2. Grain projections are Worldwatch estimates based on Census Bureau, op. cit. note 1, and on U.S. Department of Agriculture (USDA), Economic Research Service (ERS), "Production, Supply, and Demand View" (electronic database), Washington, D.C., November 1993; consumption levels for countries from FAO, *FAO Production Yearbook 1992* (Rome: 1993).
3. Grain output and projections are Worldwatch estimate based on Census Bureau, op. cit. note 1, and on USDA, op. cit. note 2; consumption levels for countries from FAO, op. cit. note 2.
4. U.N. General Assembly, "Draft Programme of Action of the International Conference on Population and Development" (draft), New York, April 1994.
5. K.S. Jayaraman, "Science Academies Call for Global Goal of Zero Population Growth," *Nature*, November 4, 1993.
6. Ibid.
7. U.N. General Assembly, op. cit. note 4.
8. Ibid.
9. Edward O. Wilson, *The Diversity of Life* (Cambridge, Mass.: Harvard University Press, 1992).
10. Robert Kaplan, "The Coming Anarchy," *Atlantic Monthly*, February 1994.
11. USDA, op. cit. note 2.
12. John Bongaarts, "Population Policy Options in the Developing World," *Science*, February 11, 1994; J. Joseph Speidel, "Population: What Does It Mean to Health?" *The PSR Quarterly*, December 1993.
13. U.S. Bureau of the Census, published in Ray Urban and Francis Nightingale, *World Population by Country and Region, 1950–1990 and Projections to 2050* (Washington, D.C.: USDA, ERS, 1993).
14. Alan Cowell, "Scientists Associated With Vatican Call for Population Curbs," *New York Times*, June 16, 1994.
15. Steven Sinding, "Getting to Replacement: Bridging the Gap

Between Rights and Demographic Goals," International Family Planning Congress, Delhi, India, October 23–25, 1992.
16. Ibid.
17. U.S. policy from Brian Dickson, Legislative Aide, Zero Population Growth, Washington, D.C., private communication, May 2, 1994.
18. Lawrence H. Summers, "Investing in *All* the People," World Bank Working Paper No. 905, Washington, D.C., May 1992.
19. Jodi L. Jacobson, *Planning the Global Family*, Worldwatch Paper 80 (Washington, D.C.: Worldwatch Institute, December 1987); Jodi L. Jacobson, *Gender Bias: Roadblock to Sustainable Development*, Worldwatch Paper 110 (Washington, D.C.: Worldwatch Institute, September 1992).

CHAPTER 16. Turning the Tide

1. United Nations, *World Population Prospects, The 1992 Revision* (New York: 1993); Population Reference Bureau, *1993 World Population Data Sheet* (Washington, D.C.: 1993).
2. Grain production from U.S. Department of Agriculture (USDA), Economic Research Service, "Production, Supply, and Demand View" (electronic database), Washington, D.C., November 1993; fish catch from U.N. Food and Agriculture Organization (FAO), *Yearbook of Fishery Statistics: Catches and Landings* (Rome: 1993).
3. Center for International Research, U.S. Bureau of the Census, "Midyear Population and Average Annual Growth Rates for the World: 1950–1995" (unpublished printout), Suitland, Md., March 25, 1993.
4. Grain prices from International Monetary Fund, *International Financial Statistics Yearbook Historical Series* (Washington D.C.: 1979); embargoes and export restrictions from Lester R. Brown, *By Bread Alone* (Washington D.C.: Praeger Publishers, 1974).
5. Robert Kaplan, "The Coming Anarchy," *Atlantic Monthly*, February 1994.
6. Population from Census Bureau, op. cit. note 3.
7. U.N. General Assembly, "Draft Programme of Action of the International Conference on Population and Development" (draft), New York, April 1994.
8. Ibid.; Table 16–1 is from Lester R. Brown and Edward C. Wolf, "Reclaiming the Future," *State of the World 1988* (New York: W.W. Norton & Company, 1988), with updates by the authors based on U.N. General Assembly, op. cit. note 7, on World Bank, *World Development Report 1992* (New York: Oxford University Press, 1992), on World Bank, *World Development Report*

1993 (New York: Oxford University Press, 1993), on Lawrence H. Summers, "Investing in *All* the People," World Bank Working Paper No. 905, Washington D.C., May 1992, and on Heinrich Von Loesch, Information Services, Consultative Group on International Agricultural Research, Washington, D.C., private communication, April 5, 1994.

9. Based on data in World Bank, *World Development Report 1993*, op. cit. note 8.
10. Number of school-age children requiring education from U.N. General Assembly, op. cit. note 7; cost of education from Summers, op. cit. note 8; number of illiterate adults from U.N. Development Programme, *Human Development Report 1993* (New York: Oxford University Press: 1993).
11. FAO, *Fuelwood Supplies in the Developing Countries*, Forestry Paper 42 (Rome: 1983).
12. Ibid.
13. Cost of establishing trees from "The Costs of a Better Environment," in World Bank, *World Development Report 1992*, op. cit. note 8, and from John S. Spears, "Replenishing the World's Forests—Tropical Reforestation: An Achievable Goal?" *Commonwealth Forestry Review*, Vol. 62, No. 3, 1983.
14. Seedling costs discussed in Dennis Anderson and Robert Fishwick, *Fuelwood Consumption and Deforestation in African Countries*, World Bank Staff Working Paper No. 704, Washington, D.C., 1984.
15. Cost of preserving U.S. cropland is a Worldwatch estimate based on data from USDA, *Agricultural Statistics 1992* (Washington D.C.: U.S. Government Printing Office, 1992).
16. Percent of degraded land from World Resources Institute, *World Resources 1994–95* (New York: Oxford University Press, 1994); cost of conserving soil from USDA, op. cit. note 15.
17. USDA, op. cit. note 15.
18. International research data from Heinrich Von Loesch, Information Services, Consultative Group on International Agricultural Research, Washington, D.C., private communication, April 13, 1994.
19. World Bank, *World Development Report 1992*, op. cit. note 8.
20. Eric Schmitt, "$261 Billion Set for the Military," *New York Times*, November 7, 1993.
21. Sandra Postel, *Last Oasis: Facing Water Scarcity* (New York: W.W. Norton & Company, 1992).
22. K.F. Isherwood and K.G. Soh, "Short Term Prospects for World Agriculture and Fertilizer Use," International Fertilizer Association, Paris, November 1993.
23. Irrigation adjustment costs from Postel, op. cit. note 20; insur-

ance companies' response from The College of Insurers, "Climate Change and the Insurance Industry: The Next Generation," Proceedings, New York, September 28, 1993.

24. United Nations Children's Fund, *The State of the World's Children 1993* (New York: Oxford University Press, 1993); U.N. General Assembly, op. cit. note 7.

25. Worldwatch estimates based on Stockholm International Peace Research Institute, *SIPRI Yearbook 1993: World Armaments and Disarmament* (Oxford: Oxford University Press, 1993).

26. U.S. intelligence spending from Tim Wirth, U.S. Department of State, Washington, D.C., private communication, September 3, 1993; UNFPA budget from S. Gythfelt, UNFPA Library, New York, private communication, April 15, 1994.

Index

ABOUT THE AUTHORS

LESTER R. BROWN is President of the Worldwatch Institute, a private, nonprofit environmental research organization in Washington, D.C. He is recipient of a MacArthur Foundation "genius award," winner of the United Nations' 1989 environment prize, and the recipient of a string of honorary degrees from universities around the world. The Library of Congress has requested Mr. Brown's personal papers and manuscripts, recognizing his role in shaping the global environmental movement. Before founding Worldwatch, he was Administrator of the U.S. International Agricultural Development Service and Advisor to the U.S. Secretary of Agriculture. He holds degrees from Rutgers University, the University of Maryland, and Harvard University. Mr. Brown started his career as a farmer, growing tomatoes in southern New Jersey.

HAL KANE is a Research Associate at the Worldwatch Institute. He is a principal author of the annual *Vital Signs: The Trends That Are Shaping Our Future* and has written or contributed to eight books on environmental subjects and numerous articles in magazines. He speaks frequently on radio shows in the United States and abroad. Prior to joining Worldwatch, Mr. Kane worked for several nonprofit environmental organizations and for the U.S. Environmental Protection Agency. He holds degrees from the University of Michigan and the Johns Hopkins University.

For Product Safety Concerns and Information please contact our EU
representative GPSR@taylorandfrancis.com
Taylor & Francis Verlag GmbH, Kaufingerstraße 24, 80331 München, Germany